EXEGESIS OF COMMONPLACES

Léon Bloy

TRANSLATED FROM THE FRENCH BY LOUIS CANCELMI

Copyright © 2021 by Wiseblood Books

Translation Copyright © 2021 by Louis Cancelmi

All rights reserved, including the right to reproduce this book or portions thereof in any form whatsoever. For information, address the publisher.

Originally published in French as *Exégèse des lieux communs* by Mercure de France, 1902.

Printed in the United States of America

Set in Baskerville Typesetting
Cover & Interior Design by Silk Studio
Interior Illustration by Helen R. Maltese
Photographic portrait of Léon Bloy (1893) by Charles Cain

ISBN-13: 978-1-951319-90-8

Wiseblood Books
Belmont, North Carolina
www.wisebloodbooks.com

Léon Bloy (1846–1917)

TRANSLATOR'S PREFACE

The work of Léon Bloy is little known in the English-speaking world, though some will have heard his name mentioned in passing, in Borges' famous essay on "Kafka and His Precursors," for example, or as a footnote in the life and literature of J.K. Huysmans. Georges Bernanos said that Bloy was the prophet of the *fin de siècle*, not one who saw the future but simply one who *saw*, and who was "the only one in this horrible crowd of gawkers to see what was there to be seen, and to stare at it unblinkingly."

The present work offers the translator many unique challenges, not the least of which being to find idiomatic English proverbs to match the original French, and, where these don't exist, to create them. Often an acceptable equivalent is ready enough to hand, only to differ in a key detail that renders it unserviceable. For instance, *"Paris n'a pas été bâti en un jour."* Perfect. "Rome wasn't built in a day" is our common and accepted version of the adage, but it won't work since, as might be supposed, Bloy isn't going to use Rome in his exegesis, he's going to use Paris. In circumstances like this, I have conserved the slightly less idiomatic version (i.e., "Paris wasn't built in a day"), supplemented a bit around the edges ("I've heard the same thing said of Rome..."), and very little if any of the effect is lost. In other cases the French may have a direct equivalent in English but conveys its meaning through divergent enough imagery that the English idiom must either be altered or abandoned altogether in order for Bloy's elaboration to make any sense. *"Qui n'entend qu'une cloche n'entend qu'un son"* (CIV) has its English analog in "There are two sides to every story," but Bloy picks up and runs with the French metaphor (literally, "If you only ever hear one bell, you'll only ever hear one sound"), which has everything to do with cacophony, sonority, and clarity, and nothing much to do with either stories or sides. My solutions to this and similar problems vary, but I have generally tried to minimize liberties taken, while preferring artistic license to impenetrability. I have also included the French original of each *lieu commun* beneath its English rendering, for reference as well as comparison.

One final matter that requires attention here is Bloy's use throughout his *Exegesis* of the epithet *Bourgeois*. He regularly employs the term as an adjective, but more often it is a noun—a person, that is, whose psyche is both the focus of and impetus for the entire undertaking. A Bourgeois, for Bloy, is not merely a conservative, middle-class, middlebrow person, though he may be all of these. He is not merely a materialistic money-grubber or businessman, though he may be those as well. Nor is the Bourgeois strictly or principally a member of the owner class or the political elite. Rather he is a *spiritual* entity, and while Bloy may despise the Bourgeois for his greed or vanity, for his hypocrisies and cruelties, nevertheless he recognizes that "in the form of *Commonplaces* the Bourgeois continually and unwittingly advances truly impressive claims, the implications of which are unknown to him…"[1] Indeed, Bloy's chief purpose with the present work is to divorce the language of the Bourgeois from its apparent or superficial meaning and lay bare its supernatural qualities.

Bloy had conceived the project of his *Exegesis* as early as 1892, more than a decade before its publication, with the insight that "the banalities these idiots never tire of trotting out all confirm, in stunning fashion, the nullity [of the bourgeoisie]; therefore they are themselves *divine*."[2] In other words, the expressions of the Bourgeois are not mere platitudes; they are also unsuspecting conduits for the Word of God, which in Bloy's theology is absolute and *cannot be falsified*. The Bourgeois is a repeater of trite phrases, just as a pious man is a repeater of prayers, and the former, not unlike the latter, often gives no special attention to what he is saying. This lack of awareness only reflects, however, a deeper truth about the human condition: that we imperfect creatures only ever see, as St. Paul maintained—and as Bloy was fond of quoting—*per speculum in aenigmate*. Nothing, from this perspective, is as it seems to be—or rather, appearance is never *only* appearance. "Everything," Bloy writes, "even the most wrenching pain, is but a *symbol*. We are dreamers, shouting in our sleep."[3] Likewise the commonplace, in Bloy's lexicology, is not merely an analog for the vacuousness of whoever spouts it but "a kind of escape hatch for fleeing whenever danger rears its head…"[4] That the Bourgeois should avail himself of such a resource is, moreover, *intrinsic* to his nature. The Bourgeois is indeed an

---

1. See XXV below.
2. Léon Bloy, *Le mendiant ingrat* (Edmond Deman: Bruxelles, 1898), p. 39.
3. *Ibid.*, p. 314.
4. See CLXXXIII below.

incarnation of the faithlessness, pride, self-justification, cleverness, obfuscation, and gluttony that mire us in the world and contaminate our relationships with others and with ourselves. But he is also, crucially,

> a senseless (but faithful) reverberation, echoing the Word of God when it rings out here in the world below. He is a dark glass reflecting fully the *mirror-image* of this same God's Face when He gazes down upon mortal waters... [To] me, there [is] something terrible in this. And that is all.[5]

—Louis Cancelmi

---

5. See XXXIV below.

NOTE FROM THE TRANSLATOR

Footnotes are mine unless otherwise indicated. Additional annotations, when not attributable to Bloy himself, were adapted or translated from those Jacques Petit (hereafter "J. P.") provided for Mercure de France's 1972 re-edition of the *Exégèse*, and have been credited accordingly. I would also like to acknowledge the profound debt my translation owes to the interventions of Trevor Cribben Merrill. Not only did he recommend me to Wiseblood Books, he generously lent his time and expertise to the revision process. His suggestions and encouragement have been invaluable in bringing this project to fruition.

"Not all died, but all had been stricken."
The Animals Sick with Plague (Jean de La Fontaine)

TO RENÉ MARTINEAU[1]

Think back, dear friend, on our little chapel of Saint Anne and Saint René, so humble and so poor, over there by the Ocean. In remembrance of this chapel and of Ker Saint-Roch's hospitality, please accept the dedication of this book—more serious and distressing than it appears—wherein I have depicted, *as I saw fit*, the evil we are dying of.

Your name here alongside mine, from this very first page, dooms you to share in my disfavor. Friend to the infamous writer whom you dared call *one of the living*, how will you escape your destiny?

That we crossed paths at all was a miracle summoned by Suffering, and it will be said without fail that our enduring friendship is another. Isn't it the most astonishing of wonders, that a man might enthusiastically free himself from those Commonplaces where proper meals are served in order to come with me and, in solitude, heroically, gnaw upon the skulls of imbeciles?

Lagny. December 31, 1901.
Léon Bloy.

---

1. René Martineau (1866–1948), writer, critic, and close friend to Léon Bloy, was the author of *Un Vivant et Deux Morts* (1901), a study of Bloy, Ernest Hello, and Villiers de l'Isle-Adam.

INTRODUCTION

I embark upon this work today, the 30th of September,[1] under the inspiration of Saint Jerome, author of the Vulgate, ostiary of all the Prophets, glorious inventory-keeper of everlasting Commonplaces.

Does this show a lack of respect for that remarkable doctor, whom the Church honors with the title *Maximus*, whom the Council of Trent implicitly declared Notary of the Holy Spirit? I don't believe it does.

Indeed, what is the purpose here, if not to pluck out the tongues of the fearsome and definitive idiots of our own century, as Saint Jerome so effectively silenced the Pelagians and Luciferians of his time?

That the Bourgeoisie be stricken dumb at last—what a dream!

I know well how insane the project must appear. Nevertheless I fully hope to carry it through, effortlessly and even enjoyably.

The true Bourgeois—that is to say, in the modern and also most general sense possible, the man who makes no use whatsoever of his intellectual faculties and who lives or appears to live without having ever been bothered, not even once, by the need to understand anything at all—the truly authentic and indisputable Bourgeois is necessarily limited in his use of language to a very small number of formulations.

The repertory of patrimonial locutions he finds sufficient is extremely meager and hardly reaches beyond a few hundred or so. Oh, that we might be blessed to relieve him of his humble treasure, what a paradise of silence then would fall upon our planet, what solace we would know!

When, for example, a government employee or a fabric-maker observes that *you can't change the way you are*; that *you can't have everything*; that *business is business*; that *medicine is a vocation*; that *Paris wasn't built in a day*; that *children don't ask to be born*, etc., etc., etc.—well, what would happen if in that same instant it were proved to him that one or another of these ancient clichés corresponded to some divine Reality, had the power to make the earth tremble and unleash catastrophes of epic proportion?

---

1. 1897, etc.

What terror wouldn't the ironmonger or publican be spared, what torments would the pharmacist and truck driver fall prey to, should they suddenly realize that they were giving voice—involuntarily—to *absolute* superfluities, that the lines they had only just spoken, in imitation of hundreds of millions of other headless folk, were in fact stolen from the Almighty Creator Himself and that, uttered at the right time, these words could very well turn a world upside-down?

What's more, a profound instinct seems to alert them to this possibility. Who hasn't noticed the cunning wariness, the solemn discretion, the *morituri sumus* of these brave fellows, when they enunciate the moldy maxims left to them by centuries of tradition, which they in turn shall transmit to their own children?

When a midwife announces that *money can't buy happiness* and the tripe-merchant responds shrewdly that *nonetheless it makes a contribution*, these two augurs have the unerring sensation of having thus exchanged precious *secrets*, of having revealed for one another some arcanum of eternal life, and their manner is commensurate with the inexpressible importance of this negotiation.

It's all too easy to speak in what appear to be commonplaces. But what a commonplace is, in actual fact, who can say?

Why otherwise would I have invoked Saint Jerome? This great character was not merely the depositary for all time of the unchanging Word, of Commonplaces thick with the Holy Trinity's thunderbolts; he was above all their interpreter and most inspired commentator.

He taught, with an authority far beyond human, that God has always spoken exclusively of *Himself*, through symbolic, parabolic, or metaphorical forms of Revelation in the Word, and that He has always, in a thousand different ways, said *the same thing*.[2]

May this sublime Doctor design to bless the undertaking of a well-meaning pamphleteer who would be only too happy to irritate, yet again, the Ninevite rabble, forever incapable of "distinguishing between their right hand and their

---

2. This is the foundation of Bloy's biblical exegesis. See, for example, chapter XX of *Le Salut par les Juifs* (1892): "In other words, the divine Word is infinite, absolute, in every way irrevocable—iterative, above all, and prodigiously so, *for God can speak only of Himself*." The connection is here clearly established between biblical exegesis and his own exegesis of Commonplaces. —J. P.

left,"³ and irritate them so thoroughly as to unleash unheard-of rages across the land.

Such would undoubtedly be the result, did heavenly gentleness not prohibit me from establishing, by irrefutable argumentation in a dialectics of solid bronze, that the most inane representatives of the bourgeoisie are themselves *fearsome prophets*—little do they know! They cannot open their mouths but the stars do shake, and from the depths of their Foolishness are conjured, instantly, chasms of Light.

---

3. Jonas 4:11. Bloy consistently cites the Vulgate or translates the Latin himself; as a best approximation, I have followed the 1914 Douay-Rheims American edition throughout.

I

EVEN GOD DOESN'T ASK SO MUCH!

Dieu n'en demande pas tant!

What an epigraph for a commentary on the Napoleonic Code! A joke so cheap, it must be left as charity for the journalists and law clerks. This is a serious matter.

It boggles the mind, doesn't it, to think that several million times a day this line is spat back in the face of a God who "asks" above all to be *eaten!* The perpetual haggling this Commonplace implies is disconcerting. It proves what a lack of appetite there is in a world nonetheless afflicted by famine and reduced to feeding on its own filth.

Now, everything in this expression (far more mysterious than one might believe) hinges on the word *much*, the abstract value of which is always at the mercy of some discretionary standard that is never revealed. Exactly *how much* depends, naturally, on the status of a given soul. Puerile of me, surely, to point that out.

But since all negation tends toward nothingness, it's not incautious to conclude that God's imprecise *demand* is equal to roughly nothing, and if in the end this God has nothing more to ask of His worshippers, who can go on scaling back their zeal indefinitely, then neither does he have much use anymore for His Own Being or Substance: he must, it follows, necessarily disappear. Indeed, it could not possibly matter less whether one has this or that notion of God. God himself *doesn't ask so much*, and that's the essential point.

When I urge my laundress, Madame Alaric, not to prostitute her youngest daughter the way she farmed out the other four, or if, in all modesty, I offer my landlord, Monsieur Dubaiser, the example of a saint or two who didn't believe it indispensable to the social equilibrium that little children be condemned to death, and if these honorable persons then reply: "We're just as religious as you are, but even God doesn't ask so much..." I must admit at least they're kind enough not to add, "On the contrary!"—even though this is obviously, necessarily, the core of their thinking.

And they're probably right, for the logic of Commonplaces is merciless. If God doesn't ask so much, then he is forced by invincible consequence to ask less and less and, ultimately, I repeat, to *refuse* everything. What am I saying? Supposing at that point he still exists even a little bit, he'll soon find himself most urgently obliged to *ask* us to live like pigs, while striking down martyrs and the pure of heart with whatever remains of his thunderbolts.

Besides, the bourgeois are too worthy of adoration not to become Gods themselves. They and they alone are the ones to whom we should address our demands. All imperatives belong to them, and we can be certain that the day they ask *too much* will be precisely the day it dawns on them that they haven't asked nearly enough…

"Dirty scoundrels!" Someone will say to them. "I'm asking for your hides!"

II

NOTHING IS ABSOLUTE

Rien n'est absolu.

Corollary to the preceding. Most men of my generation heard this throughout their childhood. Any time we went looking, drunk with disgust, for a springboard to launch us leaping and vomiting away from it all, the Bourgeois would appear before us, armed with this thunderbolt.

And so we had to return, necessarily, to a state of profitable *Relativity* and well-behaved Filth.

True, almost everyone grew accustomed to it—fortunately—and in time we became Olympian bolt-throwers ourselves.

But do they know, drunk as they are on this foul nectar, that nothing is so audacious as to countermand the Irrevocable? and that to do so implies an obligation to become *oneself* something like the Creator of a new Heaven and Earth?

Obviously, once a person's given his solemn oath that "nothing is absolute," in the same breath he's yielded the inexorability of arithmetic and sent a cloud of uncertainty to hover over the most indisputable axioms of basic geometry. All of a sudden it becomes a real question, whether it's better to slit or not to slit your father's throat; to have twenty-five pennies or seventy-four million; to have your backside kicked or to establish a dynasty.

In short, all identities give way. It isn't "absolutely" certain that this watchmaker, born the pride of his family in 1859, is today only forty-three, and that he is in fact *not* the grandfather of this old undertaker begotten during Napoleon's Hundred Days. Likewise, it would be rash to maintain that a bedbug is exclusively a bedbug and has no business aspiring to higher office.

Under such circumstances, you have to admit, there's no way around creating a world of one's own.

III

THE PERFECT IS THE ENEMY OF THE GOOD

Le Mieux est l'ennemi du Bien.

Here, I confess, the title of this collection overwhelms me, and I am mightily tempted to come down from my pulpit. *Exegesis* means, alas, *explanation*, and here is one monster of a Commonplace coming toward me on my road to Thebes. Surely no Œdipus ever had to solve so difficult a riddle as this.

But let's see.

If the Perfect is the enemy of the Good, then the Good must necessarily be the enemy of the Perfect, for philosophical abstractions have no more truck with forgiveness than with humility. A *person* might answer hate with love, but an *idea* never, and the more excellent the idea is, the deeper it digs in its heels.

What is being affirmed, then, implicitly, is that the Good loathes the Perfect, and that the two are divided by fierce hatred. It's kill or be killed, *until the end of time*. But then, who is the Good and who is the Perfect, and what was the origin of their conflict? What does this grammatical Manichaeism demand of us?

Is it *good*, for instance, to be a dunce and *perfect* to be a genius? When we say everything God has done was for the Best, i.e. in the name of Perfection, am I to understand he's done nothing for the merely Good? In what metaphysical cave did positive and superlative declare war upon one another? It's enough to drive a person crazy.

I take my head in my hands and shower myself with sweet nothings: "Let's see then! One more time, my dearest, my treasure, my little honeybunch! Just calm down, maybe we'll manage to pick up the thread." Okay, we said or heard that the Perfect is the enemy of the Good, wasn't that it? Yet if Good has an enemy, surely that would be Evil, wouldn't it? And therefore what is Perfect is identical to what is Evil. Ah, there we go, now it seems a bit of light comes shining in…

Yes, but if what is Perfect is truly Evil, we're going to be forced to recognize that what is Good is also, by the same token and quite indisputably, Evil, since everyone agrees that Good is better—that is to say *more perfect*—than Evil, which is Perfect, and that, consequently, it is better—that is again to say *more perfect*—than what is Perfect—better than what is Best—and therefore… the Worst!!!???

To hell with it! Ariadne lets me go, and I hear the Minotaur bellowing.

IV

HOSPITALS AREN'T MADE FOR DOGS

L'hôpital n'est pas fait pour les chiens.

This one—need I even say it?—is an example of *antiphrasis*. The always suave and refreshing Bourgeois readily employs this Greek form of confabulatory gloss. We shall have more than a few opportunities to remark upon it.

Here, therefore, we must read strictly: *Hospitals are made for dogs*. In this sense—the true sense—the Bourgeois speaks as a God. No mere man would be able to put it so well.

I open the *Sylva allegoriarum* of Brother Hieronymus Lauretus, scholar's folio edition, printed in Lyon in 1622 at the expense of one Barthélémy Vincent, under the sign of Victory, and at the entry for *Canis* this is what I find: "The dog is an animal of service to man, who delights in its company and caresses. It barks at strangers. It is unclean, often rageful, and extremely lubricious. It guards the herd and chases the wolves away. It is voracious and a meat-eater and will re-ingest its own vomit."

In addition to this, modern science, to which humankind owes so many useful discoveries, presumes that dogs are quadrupeds and have no means of expressing themselves through language. But there's no need to limit ourselves to these hypotheses. Besides, there are dogs and there are dogs, as everybody knows.

The dogs hospitals are made for are the meat-eaters, the unclean meat-eaters, who have grown old or infirm, whose company no longer pleases, who are no longer able to express any sort of fury, who no longer have the strength to bark, whom the pack itself is now obliged to *protect*, for the wolf's tooth threatens.

To whom else would they open their arms, I ask you, these admirable asylums where we cough up our last, no comfort spared, cradled by the Department of Social Services? The only true, authentic dog is the one who—however many paws it has left, however strong its jaws—*can no longer be made to turn a profit*. This is the dog for whom the Administration of Hooked Teats, which suckles itself on the blood of the dying, exclusively functions. The righteous Bourgeois desired it should be so.

He is the Master, isn't he? God of the living and God of the dead, yes?

Ever since the Napoleonic Code promoted him to take Jehovah's place, no one dares judge him and he does exactly as he pleases. Besides which it pleases him, it just so happens, to be Lord of the dogs.

V

POVERTY IS NO VICE

Pauvreté n'est pas vice.

Antiphrasis again. O teach me, won't you, good landlord of mine: what else might pass as *vice* or crime, if poverty is none?

I believe I've said it elsewhere many times, poverty is the *only* vice, the only sin, the exclusive black mark, the unpardonable and extra-singular form of misbehavior. That's how you understand the matter at any rate, isn't it, you precious Gluttons passing judgement on the world?

Let's proclaim it then once and for all: poverty is so odious that to confess to it would represent the highest degree of cynicism (or the final cry of a desperate conscience), and no punishment would be sufficient to expiate the crime.

So much is it the *duty* of mankind to be rich, that the presence of even a single poor person cries out to heaven like the abomination of Sodom, and strips God himself bare, forcing him to be made flesh and stroll about scandalously here on Earth, dressed only in the rags of his Prophecies.

Indigence is impious, an atrocious blasphemy whose horror is impossible to express, which in a single stroke sends both stars and dictionary stumbling backwards.

O, how the Gospels are misunderstood! When one reads that "it would be easier for a camel to pass through the eye of a needle, than for a rich man to enter into the kingdom of God," one has to be blind not to see that in reality this verse excludes only the camel—for surely every rich person, without exception, is *already* sitting upon a golden chair in Paradise, and so it follows that it is indeed entirely possible for them to enter a place they *already* occupy, and have since the beginning of time! It's the camels' business to thread needles before the pearly gates and get along as best they can. Beyond that, there's no call for concern.

More than any other this Commonplace demonstrates the sublime modesty of the Bourgeois. It is a veil thrown honestly, with the divine smile of an assistant mortician, over mankind's most purulent canker.

VI

NOBODY'S PERFECT

On n'est pas parfait.

Having made certain that the old man had been sufficiently stabbed, and that he had assuredly expelled what we are wont to call his last gasps, Asclepius Nuptial turned straightaway to contemplating where and how to procure some diversion.

This judicious fellow was of the opinion that a person ought to cut himself a little slack, and that it's wise to stop and take a breather now and then. Certainly, he liked to tell himself, every trouble is worth its reward.

He'd been lucky to get his hands on a decent sum. Happy to be alive and with a delicately deodorized conscience, he wandered here and there beneath the chestnut trees, or the sycamores, rapturously inhaling the fragrant breath of evening.

It was spring, not the equivocal and rheumatic spring of equinox, but the heady period of renewal that is early June, when the interlacing Twins of Gemini retreat before Cancer's Crab.

Asclepius, brimming with dulcet visions, eyes glistening with tears, felt himself a true apostle.

He desired happiness for the whole entire human race, brotherhood among the wild animals, protection for the oppressed, consolation for the suffering.

His heart, full of forgiveness, held a special fondness for the destitute. He lavished upon their outstretched hands the abundant copper coins that weighed his pockets down.

He even went into a church and joined a flock of the faithful in their recitation of the common prayer. He praised God, telling Him he loved his neighbor as himself. He gave thanks for the goods he had received, acknowledging that he himself had been fashioned from nothing.

He asked that the darkness that concealed from him the ugliness and corruption of sin be lifted. He made a scrupulous examination of his conscience, and discovered in himself enduring imperfections, persistent trifles: transports of vanity, moments of impatience and distraction, faults of omission, harsh and uncharitable judgments, etc., but above all laziness and negligence in carrying out the *duties of his station.*

He concluded by resolving to be less fragile from here on out; he implored the assistance of Heaven for travelers and for the dying; he asked, as is proper, to be protected during the night; and, infused with these fine sentiments, he hustled directly to the nearest whorehouse.

For he believed in honest pleasures. He wasn't one to give himself over just like that to frivolous debaucheries. On the contrary, he erred ever on the side of rigor and was very nearly a caricature of his own seriousness.

He killed in order to live—as most honest people do—because there's no such thing as a stupid job.[1] He could have gone about, as so many others did, boasting the dangers of this rather ticklish profession. But he preferred silence. The flowers of his soul, like the trumpet-petaled convolvulus, blossomed only in the half-light.

He did his killing at home, politely, discreetly, and as cleanly as can be imagined. You might say it was difficult work, ably executed.

He made no promises he wasn't able to keep. In fact, he made no promises at all. But his clients never expressed dissatisfaction.

As for the gossipmongers, he paid them no mind. *Do right and fear no man,* that was his motto. The vote of his own conscience was suffrage enough for him.

The truth is, he was a homebody, and was only rarely to be met in the cafés; even those who wished him ill were forced to admit that, outside of the brothel, he hardly saw anyone at all.

It was in that hospitable dwelling that his affections lit upon a scantily-dressed young girl, by whose talents the establishment thrived, and whose precocious virtuosity made her an object of enthusiasm. She was scarcely more than a child, and already she was, in numerous salons, a subject of admiration.

Lucky Asclepius had a gift for making people love him, and O time seemed to "suspend its flight"[2] when these two beings were pining each for the other across the enchanted lake.

The ravishing Loulou forgot everything else as soon as her little Cucu

---

1. See CLXIV below.

2. Alluding to *Le lac*, a poem by Alphonse de Lamartine, and one of the more famous verses in French poetry: *Ô temps, suspends ton vol!*

appeared, and when the old gents started to get impatient, he was often forced to bring her back, with a firm hand, to the professional bearing her art required. In return she would supply him certain precious bits of information...

In short, they savvily managed to stack up some rather attractive sums. Loulou spent next to nothing, air and light sufficing for her daily *toilette,* always simple as can be and in perfect taste.

They could already glimpse their reward, the happy future awaiting them in the countryside, in a cottage they would buy someday, burrowed among roses and lilac trees, and that peaceable old age which Providence holds in store for those who have put up a noble fight.

Yes, very likely, but alas! Can anyone measure the vanity of human thought?

What follows is altogether too painful.

That night, Asclepius failed to show up. This caused the house more distress than can be described. Poor Loulou, restless at first, then agitated, and finally distraught, stopped putting out altogether.

A Belgian lawyer who had brought along his clients' funds was greeted with a pair of resounding slaps, to the astonishment of passers-by.

The scandal was enormous, and a general outcry seemed imminent. But she refused to listen to "anything or anybody." Her anxiety had progressed to delirium, and in her contempt for the law she went so far as to open a window that had remained shut since Bastille Day the previous year. With a dreadful voice she called out for her Cucu, through the great nocturnal silence.

A few Protestant pastors took flight, not without expressing their indignation, and already the following day serious newspapers were gloomily prognosticating the end of the world.

Do I have to spell it out? Asclepius was out carousing, Asclepius had met a snake.

He had been on his way back to the cradle of love, like a good little boy, when he was accosted by a childhood schoolmate he hadn't seen for ten years. The latter managed to corrupt him, for the first time in his life.

I don't know exactly which sophisms this gruesome friend deployed in order to turn our Asclepius from the straight and narrow path that leads to heaven, but they got so drunk that, with dawn approaching, wailing Loulou's wide-eyed lover took a coach to go retrieve a copy of Scupoli's *Spiritual Combat* he remembered having forgotten at his corpse's residence the day before, and which he deemed absolutely indispensable to his inner development.

His faithful companion that night guided him, as though by the hand, all the way to the dead man's bedroom, where the chief of police obligingly awaited.

And so a single fault ruined two careers.

Nobody's perfect.[3]

---

3. The touching story you've just had the pleasure of reading is not, unfortunately, appearing here for the first time. It was slipped into my *Disagreeable Tales,* published by Dentu in 1894. The failure of that book (which remains almost entirely unknown) was so tremendous that, with the exception of a few madmen who collect my every pencil shaving, we can be certain no one's ever read this passage before. Besides, why reinvent the wheel, when it has already been so well-crafted? What other, more luminous gloss could I possibly have given this phrase? [Bloy's note in the original edition. —TRANS.]

VII

INDECENT PEOPLE FEAR THE LIGHT

Les malhonnêtes gens redoutent la lumière.

And as for the decent ones! Does anyone think light gives them comfort? Indeed, had light yet to be created, I don't know what this or that rascal would do—but I know well what decent people *wouldn't*.

No one sees very clearly on this planet of ours, not yet anyway; here even the most clear-sighted can only feel their way around. It appears, however, that this little light is already too much, since everyone is hiding. What would happen if Science, so admired by Zola and so worthy of the admiration of such a brain, came and cast a brand new *ray* that illuminated the hollows of our hearts?

Isn't it obvious that in that instant every sort of business would become impracticable, impossible? No more commerce, no more industry, no more political alliances, no more medicine, no more drugstores, no more cooking, no more trials, no more marriages, no more burials, no more wills, no more "good works" of any kind. And finally, no more love. *Decent people would cease to be born...* The only ones left to look after the general bustle of humanity would be those who "fear the light" and whom we call indecent. What strange disorder!

It's true, too, that soon enough the latter would succumb in turn, having by force of circumstance become decent people themselves, to take the place of those who had disappeared—and so the two species that make up the totality of our genus would disappear, exterminated one after the other by *the light*, like those bright, fresh colors which, they say, the sunshine eats for luncheon.

Let's hope these misfortunes don't come to pass, and that indecent people as well as decent ones—those who "fear" the light no less than those who merely find it indiscreet—will continue to repel one another beneath the pale blue sky, jointly demonstrating their mutual value in the poetic setting of bailiffs, police officers, and greenery. Universal harmony demands it.

VIII

CHILDREN DON'T ASK TO BE BORN

Les enfants ne demandent pas à venir au monde.

Monsieur Paul Bourget,[1] a eunuch by vocation and one of our most illustrious adepts of the Commonplace, has gone to the trouble of recommending this one. I won't offend my readers by reminding them of the powerful book whose spine bears this very slogan.

It appears quite certain indeed, that even children *don't ask so much*. It's their way of keeping close to a state of divinity, and this is probably why they occasionally manage to appeal to the religious Bourgeois soul, which reserves its deepest adoration for whatever asks nothing of it at all.

I confess, there's something troubling in the very idea of a child asking to be born, and it helps me better understand the prophet Jeremiah's lament, that his mother hadn't remained eternally pregnant with him, never able to give birth. That said, if we're talking about being born a Bourgeois… or a Psychologist, then impatience might, strictly speaking, start to make sense.

As an axiom, therefore, this Commonplace doesn't seem acceptable to me, and I'm afraid Paul may have let himself be drawn further than necessary down the path of dues collector—or overly zealous head clerk of the civil registry. I'm almost ready even to join the foul Schopenhauer in believing that all children do, without exception, *ask* to be born, and that this might go some way toward explaining the irrational transports of love.

It goes without saying that, in this particular matter, I've absolutely forbidden myself to include or even hint at religious ideas (involving such things as Divine Prescience or Predestination), which any perspicacious Bourgeois would disdain. Saint Columban, it is said, could hear the cries of little children calling out from their mother's wombs. My barber has never heard anything like that, and all this supernatural business has been more than sufficiently debunked by the advent of the bicycle.

Restricting myself to the hypothetical allegation of the aforementioned

---

1. Celebrated Catholic novelist Paul Bourget (1852–1935), frequent target of Bloy's anti-bourgeois spleen. Under attack here specifically is the preface to his popular 1892 novel, *La Terre promise*.

pedant,[2] I think it fitting to venture that if children, even Bourgeois children, don't literally ask to be born, they do seem to suggest (at least to their parents) an instinctive horror of the virginity or continence that would disallow their entry into life… I don't know if I'm making myself understood. In any case, this would suffice to invalidate the slogan.

But when a notary affirms, accompanying his pronouncement with a bilateral gesticulation, that "children don't ask to be born," in practical terms this can only mean one of two things: either that one must give up making them, or else that they should be killed before they are born, in the interest of families and, to be sure, in the interest of potential heirs. Never—may the sky itself crumble and fall—never ever must it get around, for example, that some little bastard dropped from a beggarwoman's belly has any right whatsoever to the mercy of a procreator he is forever forbidden to seek out. And that's the whole of it: the precise whole.

Try and tell yourself, after this, that our lovely world was redeemed, nineteen centuries ago, by a Child who had been asking to be born for all Eternity!

---

2. *i.e.* Bourget.

IX

YOU HAVE TO EAT IF YOU'RE TO LIVE

Il faut manger pour vivre.

"All I ask," says some poor devil, "is something to eat. Life may not be sweet for me, nevertheless I have to put something between my teeth. Every dog eats and lives. And those who aren't so lucky as to have a master serve them feed just the same on excellent garbage, quite sufficient to sustain their doggish existence. Not me, though. I can't. I have the misfortune of belonging to the human race, and of having been blessed with a noble brow that must remain ever fixed upon the stars. I don't have much of a sense of smell, and carrion is indigestible to me…"

I've heard it said that, once upon a time, there was a Meat for the poor, and that someone dying of hunger could resort to eating God and thereby go on living eternally. Long, long ago, one would crawl, weeping tears of Paradise, from the confessor's chapel to a martyr's crypt, from a miraculous sanctuary to a basilica full of glory, along roads jammed full of pilgrims begging for the Savior's Body. This unique food *sufficed* for a Blessed few, whose weariness had the power to heal all weariness and even, now and then, resuscitate the dead. This is all far away now, terribly far away…

Today, the Bourgeois has taken the place of Jesus, and even hungry sows recoil at the offering of his body!

X

YOU CAN'T LIVE WITHOUT MONEY

On ne peut pas vivre sans argent.

True, true. In-di-spu-ta-bly. So much so that, when you don't have any yourself, you're *forced* to take the money others have. Which can be done, by the way, in perfectly good faith.

"It's not like I'm putting a gun to anyone's head," points out the affable loan shark charging fifty percent interest. "I'm the one taking the risk, and *the money has to be put to work.*" Living without money is as inconceivable to this equitable man as living without God would be for a hermit in the Thebaid. And both of these pleasure-seekers are right, since their object is *identical*, inexpressibly IDENTICAL.

Having already thoroughly proven that it is impossible to live without eating, it's more or less pointless to undertake demonstrating the vital necessity of money. Hardworking fathers cry out all together: *Our money is being eaten up!* Oh, what an illuminating stroke, this metonymic locution!

But tell me, what do you expect a person to eat, if not money? What else in the world is there that's edible?

Isn't it clear as day that Money is precisely this same God who wants us to devour Him, who is the only source of life, the living Bread, the saving Bread, the Wheat of the elect, the Food of Angels, but also, at the same time, the hidden Manna which poor people seek in vain?

It's true that your Bourgeois, who otherwise knows almost everything, fails to penetrate this mystery. It's also true that the meaning of the verb "to live" isn't clear to him, since the money without which (as he so generously maintains) a person cannot live, is nevertheless, for him, a MATTER *of life or death...*

So what? He's got money, that's the essential thing. If he doesn't eat it himself, others will eat it when he's gone, that's for sure.

But I challenge him, when he utters these dreadful words, to do so *without* looking like a true prophet or attesting to the infinite almightiness of God. *Trahitur sapientia de occultis.*[1]

---

1. "Wisdom is drawn out of secret places." (Job 28:18)

XI
PUT YOUR MONEY TO WORK
Faire travailler l'argent.

As we've just seen, this Commonplace springs forth from the preceding as the bee springs forth from a flower. The oft-repeated precept that you should put your money to work is far more *theological*, at bottom, than economic, as a necessary consequence of the identity I've just recorded.

To work, in the sense of the Latin term *laborare*, is TO SUFFER. Money, therefore, which is God, is being made to suffer. And it is made to suffer, naturally, the most abundant indignity. With the exception of spitting—since for the Bourgeois "money is nothing to spit at"—money is spared no scorn. It is even made to *sweat*. It is made to sweat the blood of poor people laboring themselves miserably to death.

Whole populations polish themselves off in factories or lightless catacombs in order to soften the mouths of virgins engendered by top-notch capitalists, and so that "the mysterious smile of *La Gioconda*" may not be denied them. That's what's called *putting your money to work!*

...And the PALE Face of Christ is paler still at the bottom of a well, or in a blazing furnace.

XII

BUSINESS IS BUSINESS

Les affaires sont les affaires.

Respectable and austere as these Commonplaces tend to be, this one, I think, is the gravest and most venerable of the lot. It is the very umbilicus of Commonplaces, this century's highest example of platitudinous speech. But it must be understood, and such understanding is not given indiscriminately to all men. Neither poets, for example, nor artists quite comprehend it. Those to whom we refer anachronistically as heroes or even saints don't grasp it at all.

Spiritual business, the business of salvation, the business of honor, the business of state, even civic business, these are all sorts of business that could just as easily be other things, but they are *not* the sort of Business that can only be Business, without distinction or qualification.

To be in Business is to be in the Absolute. An absolute businessman is himself a sort of stylite, who never descends from his column. He must have neither thoughts, nor feelings, nor eyes, nor ears, nor nose, nor taste, nor touch, nor indeed stomach for anything but Business. The businessman recognizes neither father nor mother nor uncle nor aunt nor wife nor children, knows neither beauty nor ugliness nor cleanliness nor dirtiness nor heat nor cold nor God nor demon. He is hopelessly ignorant of all literature, art, science, history, law. He must know and recognize Business alone.

"You may have the Sainte-Chapelle and the Louvre over there in Paris, but here in Chicago we kill eighty thousand hogs a day!" Spoken like a true businessman. And yet there are truer businessmen still—for example, the fellow who sells this pig flesh. And this pork-seller is superseded in turn by a shrewd buyer who floods the European markets with it.

It would be impossible to say precisely what Business is. It's something like the boorish man's Isis, a mysterious divinity who supplants all other gods and goddesses. Nor would it tear away her Veil to include mention here, or elsewhere, of money, gambling, ambition, etc. Business is Business, no less than God is God—that is to say, separate and apart from everything else. Business is Inexplicable, Unprovable, Uncircumscribable, to such a degree that the mere pronouncement of this Commonplace is enough to decide any question, to muzzle, instantly, any blame, anger, complaint, supplication, indignation, or recrimination. One has only to utter these Five Syllables and everything has been said, every answer has been given, and there is no further Revelation to be hoped for.

In a word, those who seek to penetrate this arcanum are summoned to a kind of mystical detachment, and the time is probably not too far away when men will flee all the vanities and pleasures of this world to hide in solitude, where they may dedicate themselves entirely, exclusively, to BUSINESS.

XIII

THE LAW IS ON MY SIDE

J'ai la loi pour moi.

It was an old-fashioned Christian family. The father, an excellent worker, salt of the earth, always brought every penny of his wages home. The mother, a valorous soul, kept the house in order. The oldest child, a handsome young man of fourteen years, had just begun his apprenticeship, and the two little girls—the elder of whom was getting ready for her first communion—went to the nuns for their schooling. They were humble people, guileless in the extreme, who wanted to become saints. The smallest trifle flung upon their good intentions would not have fallen to the ground.

They prayed together, every morning and every evening. They all went to mass together, on Sundays and feast days and, as often as possible, to an early morning service during the week. More than once they would have read Crespin's *History of the Martyrs*, or one of those other rare, life-giving books. A few pious images, repellent but touching, hung on the walls: a *Seated Virgin* crushed under fifteen hundred lithographic stones, a Guido Reni *Ecce Homo*, colorized by barbaric glaziers, a tasteful *Golgotha* and a *Holy Family* stripped of serenity, which someone had picked up at the carnival.

But the most honored, most venerated picture depicted a horselike and tutelary Leo XIII. For these poor folk the atrocious caricature was the very presence, not exactly of the Son of God, but of his Vicar. Beside it they had hung a pink nightlight that was always lit, and for which there was a rule not to pass by it without saying a prayer.

You never saw more pious Christians. Their devotion to the Pope—in their eyes the Father of fathers—was something unique, perfectly simple, almost majestic. They would have given their mortal lives and several centuries of eternal peace, anything and everything that could be given, to spare the Sovereign Pontiff the smallest concern, the most innocent affront.

Misfortune befell the family, and they were abandoned like lepers. The father was smashed up by a machine while the boss looked on, later claiming no responsibility. Their landlord's *unknown* property manager moved to have them evicted, though not without holding on to the furniture, right down to the famous icon of Saint Peter's Successor. The mother, for her part, died of heartbreak and toil. As for the young man, when he turned up again four years later, he'd become a judge of his own times—and pimp to his own two sisters.

He happened to know that the landlord who put the final touches on their downfall by kicking them out *in accordance with the law* was a foreigner by the name of Pecci,[1] and that he occupied the Holy See in Rome, to say nothing of the one that remains in the hands of infidels, in Antioch, where the disciples of Jesus were first called Christians.

Yes, Most Holy Father, the LAW is on your side.

Post-scriptum. Since no law, however theophobic, obliges me to offend the weak (not so far, at least), I hereby make it known, once and for all, that I have a certain penchant for expressing myself in *parable*, and that the preceding is, manifestly, a case in point. Obviously, I wouldn't be able to give the address of any rental property belonging to Leo XIII, but I could name *all* the parish churches of France which Innocent III, say, or Gregory IX would long since have placed under Interdict for the sole and monstrous fact (which horribly compromises the Vicar of the poor man's God) that anyone who enters them Barefoot is invariably and shamefully *evicted*.

---

1. *i.e.* Leo XIII.

XIV
YOU CAN'T HAVE EVERYTHING
On ne peut pas tout avoir.

No doubt, no doubt, and especially when the law is already on your side, as we've just been saying. To ask for the rest besides, why, you might as well seek to swallow the entire world! Yet the Bourgeois is God-like, *even he doesn't ask so much.* Contemptuous of whatever is Infinite or Absolute, he knows how to set his own limits. Indeed, who could know better than he? After all, hasn't it been his unique concern, the work to which he's devoted his every hour, since childhood—to plant boundary markers everywhere?

And note how modest this Commonplace is. It doesn't say, "You *shouldn't* have everything," but rather, "You *can't.*" The Bourgeois should have everything, since everything belongs to him, but he can't take hold of everything, can't enfold it all in his—alas!—too little arms. "The misery of a great lord," wrote Pascal, "the misery of a king dethroned."[1]

When I ask my grocer for something he doesn't typically carry, and he replies with a hearty smile, "You can't have everything," this honorable man might think he's only let slip a humble burp. What I hear, though, is the monstrous groaning of Prometheus...

Not to have everything! What misfortune! And yet this phrase, which resembles a supernatural recrimination and which is launched relentlessly from millions of sublime voice boxes targeting the stars, has yet to break anything in heaven! I wonder... how can it be?

---

1. *i.e.* "All these miseries are proof, even, of his greatness." See Pascal's *Pensées* (Brunschvicg 398): *Toutes ces misères-là même prouvent sa grandeur. Ce sont misères de grand seigneur, misères d'un roi dépossédé.* —J. P.

XV

WE CAN'T ALL BE RICH

Tout le monde ne peut pas être riche.

Apparently less absolute than the preceding, this one has the advantage of being more precise. On the merits, the two are perfectly identical. It therefore made sense to bring them together, to put them in contact, pointing up the fact that both arouse the same thoughts and feelings.

For it is time we say it plainly: this most astonishing of languages, the language of Commonplaces, shares with the language of the Prophets the marvelous characteristic of *always saying the same exact thing*. Members of the bourgeoisie, who enjoy the privilege of this language, and who, like those sages who've reduced their intellectual functioning to the barest minimum, are able to draw on only a very limited number of ideas, necessarily encounter each one of these at every intersection of their quincunx, at each spin of the bobbin. I pity anyone who fails to feel the beauty in that. When a bourgeois woman says, for example, "I don't go around with my head in the clouds," you can be sure this is all she means to say, that this says it all and she's said all there is, absolutely and forevermore.

"Not everyone can be rich." Those five words don't seem like much, do they? And in reality they're even less: they're nothing—but just try replacing them! You want to express this forceful idea in a new way, that not everyone can have a large number of hundred dollar bills in his pocket, which is to say, not everyone can be a member of the bourgeoisie (they can't have everything, that's understood; all the same, they do have money). You want to destroy this Commonplace by uncovering some form that's never been used before. Well, go ahead and get searching then, get digging and hunting, turn the world upside down. You might come across the *Iliad*, but you won't find *that!* It's enough to make you weep with admiration.

XVI

DIE RICH

Il faut mourir riche.

This is a Belgian expression, really, but such a lovely one! And anyway, it's destined to become French, once France finally annexes this spiritual population for itself—oh, happy day!

To die rich! An heroic wish! A prodigious desideratum! What are the commandments of God, the commandments of the Church, the Sufferings of the Redeemer, the Compassion of the Blessed Mary, the blood of eighteen million Martyrs, and the ecstasies of the Saints, beside this? Paradise is to die a fat swine, as Saint Paul himself would have been forced to acknowledge, had he known the Belgians.

In light of this grandiose Commonplace which so aptly expresses the soul of a people, I'm almost ashamed and half-fearful to continue my Exegesis. Poor as an old rat and fated in all probability to die like one, how can I hope to contend with such formidable arcana? Where do I find the audacity to press at such length on these foreboding topics, which always seem on the verge of unleashing a thunderbolt? My sense is I'm fiddling around with a most terrible explosive device. Who are these fearsome bourgeois, who manage to utter such phrases, routinely, exclusively, from dawn till dusk, without perishing of fright?

Post-scriptum. The Bourgeois are invincibly persuaded that Trappist monks, *who have taken a vow never to speak*, never cross one another's path without saying, "Brother, remember, you must die." It's one of their most cherished ideas. It reminds me of that famous tomb every monk is obliged to dig, every day, for his own personal use, eight hours a day, for the whole duration of his religious life, which is to say, sometimes, fifty years or more. The Bourgeois is the Cynaegeirus[1] of these two boats. He won't let go of either one.

But to return to the first: I only meant that in Belgium there is probably an addition to be made to the French text. What the Belgian Trappists should be whispering is, "Brother, remember, you must die *rich.*"

---

1. Cynaegeirus was a Greek warrior (and brother of the poet Aeschylus), who during the Battle of Marathon had both hands cut off trying to hold on to the stern of a Persian ship. Legend has it that, rather than submit, he fought on, hanging from the boat by his teeth. —J. P.

XVII

WHEN YOU'RE RUNNING THE STORE...

Quand on est dans le commerce...

It took me a while to get around to it. This frequently employed phrase is recommended above all for its extreme nobility. To be running the store means, among the bourgeois, to be sitting on an immense golden throne, ready to pass judgment upon the world. An aristocracy beside which all aristocracies amount to not quite rubbish. Grandees and peeresses would consider themselves most-humbly honored to serve such an authority, were things in their rightful place. As for the artists, and those last few wretches who still make use of their faculty of thought, who can say to what low uses they must be put? But have patience.

To be running the store! Now there's an answer to everything, there's something that takes every privilege, every available favor, every imaginable exemption, every amnesty into account. What is forbidden to everyone, everywhere, at all times, becomes not only lawful but even professional—when you're running the store. The famous speech of Esther's great King, "This law is not made for thee, but for all others,"[1] appears to have been spoken on behalf of those who are running the store, whom- and wherever they may be.

What is being sold is of little importance. Whether cheese, wine, horses, jewelry, trinkets, wedding wreaths, rotting carcasses, or scraps of this or that, so long as it sells, or even if it's just for sale, with no chance of being sold, and there are some transaction ledgers behind it, with an openwork counter like you'd see in a shapely little shopping arcade—that's all that matters.

Lying, stealing, poisoning, pimping, prostitution, treason, sacrilege and apostasy are all honorable, when you're running the store. "You prostrate yourself before the customer," I overheard the owner of a café say to one of her waiters. "Face down on your belly. Always face down on your belly when you're running the store." This recommendation—what am I saying?—this *precept*, which, in other circumstances, would have represented the lowest level of ignominy, was in this instance something like an omen, resembled nothing so much as a prophecy. I've seen few gestures to approach the majesty of this cashier, swelled up with enthusiasm, her snout held high, her index finger extended imperiously toward the floor, in the same painterly

---

1. Esther 15:13.

pose as an Elisabeth Tudor pointing to the block upon which Mary Stuart was to lay her head. I was given a glimpse that day, as in a flash of light, of the mysterious and incommunicable beauty of Running the Store.

Don't get me wrong. Something sells, or can be sold, depending on whether there is an immediate taker or not. This something could be a head of lettuce, some medication, a pocket knife, a soldier's whore, what you will. The seller is always a prodigious man, a thaumaturge with the power to give to God the Father what belongs to the Holy Spirit, that is to say, to make Love pass through Faith and Fire through Water, which can hardly be made sense of at all.

And yet it's quite simple. Money, which is what makes this transposition possible, is the Redeemer—or, if you like, the image of the Redeemer. But there you have it! Shopkeepers, by nature hermetic, are equally indifferent to the Redeemer, to Redemption, to the Three Theological Virtues of Faith, Hope, and Love, to the Three Persons of the Divine Trinity, and, in general, to everything that may be conceived of by human understanding.

How many times have I been counseled to "do something that sells"? In other words, to write like a pig in order to get rich—alas!

XVIII

YOU CAN'T CHANGE THE WAY YOU ARE

On ne se refait pas.

It's something a discouraged phoenix might say. You'll hear it from gamblers, too, sometimes, but without conviction. I hereby confess my confusion.

Does the Bourgeois really think you can't change the way you are, that you can only change other people, or mustn't we believe there's some irony at work here? Irony—not likely. It doesn't fit with the pretentious gravitas. He must truly think you can't change the way you are, which seems like a harsh conclusion. But how does he understand it? That's the question. You always have to expect some surprise from him, some unforeseen revelation that will throw you to the ground and knock you out, from which it will be difficult to pick yourself back up again.

Let's set aside straightaway the negative hypothesis of restoring old carcasses, favored by notaries and professional tailors. The Bourgeois is too enlightened not to recognize the progress of science, of which he is the preordained Benefactor. He knows that science never rests, that it will never rest, and that, tomorrow perhaps, it will light the fire again beneath old Aeson's pot—rediscovered at last! This, surely, isn't what our Bourgeois would be so bold as to deny.

What's left? And what impossible renewal is he talking about then? Oh, how inscrutable the Bourgeois mind! I've spent a good part, likely the most beautiful part, of my existence trying to find the meaning of this Commonplace. I've come up with absolutely nothing so far, and, well, I'd rather just tell you plainly: I've given up looking.

XIX

MEDICINE IS A VOCATION

La médecine est un sacerdoce.

Oh, these vocations, these sacred callings! Who will attempt to enumerate them all? The vocation of agriculture, of the judiciary, of pharmacology, greengrocery, bureaucracy, politics, teaching. The vocation of swordsmanship, the vocation of journalism, etc., and finally the ancient vocation of Prostitution, lately restored to its rightful honor. Pretty much the only vocation that isn't one anymore is the religious vocation, having been formally and quite judiciously stricken from the list by the Bourgeois, who after all knows from vocations, being himself responsible for having instituted all our contemporary ones.

I singled out medicine, without really thinking about it, because that's the first vocation that came to mind and, you have to admit, it's an excellent choice.

A doctor who sniffs thirty or forty Bourgeois chamber pots and feels up their private viands every morning before breakfast cuts a different figure than a missionary announcing the word of God to poorly brought-up idolators who might eat him after his sermon, there's just no way around it. And the wording of a prescription is something altogether different from a bishop's mandate—isn't it?

I wonder anyway what becomes of the liturgies, the ecclesiastical canons, next to the tappings, fiddlings, and examinations of doctors, or in comparison with their isochronic and stereotypical slogans, falling from on high, which they never fail to deliver?

When someone asserts that medicine is a vocation, tell yourself with pious humility that behind this clergy there necessarily stands an ineffable and almighty God, and that it is your responsibility to disentangle Him, as far as you are able, from all the other Gods—no less ineffable and no less powerful—who are themselves situated behind other, innumerable clergies. These vocations, these sacred callings!

XX

ALL OPINIONS ARE TO BE RESPECTED
Toutes les opinions sont respectables.

"So long as they're sincere," added the fishmonger with a wink.

"Naturally," resumed the cheerful proprietress of the *Golden Horn*—she'd just purchased a putrefying little catch for her boarders. "You see, I'm all for liberty. Every man for himself and the Good Lord for us all."

"You can say that again! Well put! So how about it, you don't want any of my mussels? I'll give 'em to you for a song, have to get rid of them anyway."

"No, no, thanks, I have to check on my soup, you know, I left it on the stove." And the honorable hostess, who did, come to think of it, seem impatient to get back, was on her way again as quickly as her plump form— and the weight of a giant net laden with provisions—allowed.

For twenty years Madame Zola had been running a twelfth-rate furnished hotel, to which was attached a rather ghastly restaurant. The *Golden Horn*, situated in the vicinity of Val-de-Grâce, appeared to have a clientele of poor young folk, but the hourly and even shorter-term renting of nearly all the rooms proved handsome compensation for the landlady, who would have been indignant and shocked, just shocked, if anyone had told her the house was a brothel.

It was said she'd been something of a hot number once upon a time, back when the late Vallès was still a youth, and had slipped the firing squad by hitching up her skirt somewhat further than the astonished soldiers could bear. Word was she'd drummed a gas can and swallowed fire—not without virtuosity—beneath her share of balconies of a warm spring night. Which was probably the reason she wanted all opinions to be respected. It was something she absolutely insisted upon.

"Where is that little pig?" she asked when she arrived.

"Saw him scampering off more than an hour ago—toward the church, as usual. He hasn't been back since." This was Ferdinand, the waiter.

"Oh, didn't I know it! It's always church with him, always mass, always that Blessed Lord of his! Christ! It's so aggravating! I've a good mind to throw him out for good, if he ever comes back."

The little pig was a simple bugger of thirty-five years or so. In financial ruin thanks to some clever speculations, he was living off a humble job and, drawn in by the modest rent, had thought it a good idea to board up at the *Golden Horn*. The man had been raised well—a kind of monster more or less unknown among our later generations and which, excepting a few Anglo-Saxon animal trainers, will soon have gone extinct. He was even devoutly religious, a possibility beyond Madame Zola's faculties of comprehension, which threw her for an absolute loop.

It will be said she could have taken it in stride, could have taken refuge in indifference—ah, but no! No, she couldn't. Her heart had been stolen, ravaged. It had become this half-centenarian's dream to end up in her boarder's arms. The heroine of '71 longed to season her aging flesh with this one last love.

Seeing this poor object, silent and sad, and knowing herself to be a past master of consolation, she told herself the job was already done. How hard could it be to seize hold of such an unfortunate soul? But then here comes his bloody religion, getting in her way! No way of fooling herself about that: she could never walk the Good Lord's path, and neither could her business, and this Jesuit would jump ship as soon as he realized a whore was in love with him!

That very morning, in fact, she had resolved to bring this process to a conclusion, analogous perhaps to the one that once upon a time had disarmed MacMahon's *culottes rouges*.[1] And here the wretch had gone a-worshipping, without seeming to suspect a thing. So he hadn't seen anything after all, hadn't understood! Oh, for goodness' sake! it wasn't as though she'd thrown herself around his neck, or gotten down on her knees, which would have been decisive (or would have been, at least, for the old stools at the *Golden Horn*, for Madame Zola weighed in at close to three hundred kilos). But the little attentions she'd directed at him, the sweet nothings, the canoodling, the barely disguised and endlessly repeated advances from one minute to the next, so many looks and smiles, shouldn't all of this have clued him in? Alas! Full of such painful thoughts, she set about mechanically opening the letter a messenger had just handed her.

---

1. Referring to the French army's uniform during the Franco-Prussian war. MacMahon was forced to surrender at the Battle of Sedan, which proved the decisive victory for Germany.

"Dearest Lady," the message read, "Please leave the suitcase you will find in my room with the porter. The extreme sorrow my leaving you causes me is happily assuaged by the hope that it will give your soul some peace, concealing the titillating beauty of my face from your all-too-pure eyes. Oh, most tender and most incendiary Zola, I respect you every bit as much as an opinion, any one of these innumerable opinions, always old and always so young, which you so often recommend that we respect. Farewell, then, O Emily: your image is immovably anchored in my heart. ALPHONSE ALLAIS, *chemist 1ˢᵗ class (retired)*."[2]

"The sanctimonious little prig!" vociferated our gentle hostess, who didn't know quite what else to say. For a bourgeoise to be mistaken, why, it simply never happens.

---

2. Alphonse Allais (1854–1905), poet and humorist, and friend of Léon Bloy from his days at *Le Chat noir*.

XXI

I'LL BELIEVE IT WHEN I SEE IT
(LIKE SAINT THOMAS)...

Je suis comme Saint Thomas...

You've all known a stay-at-home Sicamber like this, declaring his independence through skepticism. He's like St. Thomas. He needs to see and touch something before he can believe in it. For it's natural enough (isn't it?) that St. Thomas the Apostle, dubbed the *Twice-deep Abyss* by the Holy Spirit, should be appraised according to present-day common sense and measured with maximal precision, following the irreproachable methods of psychological evaluation established by the likes of Paul Bourget to confirm his unshakeable Bourgeois posture.

No man of average intelligence will hesitate to recognize Saint Thomas as the patriarch of positivists, that is to say, of men without faith and even—to put all our cards on the table—of a rather large number of miscreants who, by misfortune, worm their way into this band of luminaries, whatever precautions one might take.

But there's something quite beautiful here that tends to go unsaid. Which is that the disciple has surpassed the master and that the Bourgeois is much greater than Saint Thomas ever was. Indeed, the admirable superiority of the Bourgeois consists in not believing even *after* having seen and touched. But no, it's more than that! By not believing he has even become *incapable* of seeing or touching. Here we find ourselves on the threshold of Infinity.

A famous visionary once said it was the finger of Saint Thomas that made the world go round—this finger which penetrated the Wounded Hands of Christ. It's terrifying to imagine what bodies might be set in motion by an individual greater than Saint Thomas, and who only thinks himself his equal!

XXII

I WASH MY HANDS OF IT (LIKE PILATE)

Je m'en lave les mains, comme Pilate.

Another allusion to the Gospels—and surely not the last. The Bourgeois isn't religious, exactly, but like a faithful boot-scraper or a long- and well-used doormat he's full of accumulated remnants, all more or less distinct. Nothing seems easier to him than to doubt like Saint Thomas and, at the same time, like Pilate, to wash his hands of this or that.

Traditionally and instinctively, Pilate is the Bourgeois hero of choice. Of all the characters in the Gospel, he speaks most directly to the bourgeois heart—in him it has discovered its prototype! Maybe the Bourgeois doesn't know this story all that well, and, probably, the reason for this famous hand-washing isn't especially familiar to him. He has better things to worry about, but still…

Their ancestors, the old bourgeois, long since returned to dust, could well have known this gesture as a metaphorical plea of innocence. The Bourgeois of today, ultra-modern and, consequently, better armed against all kinds of notions, has judiciously expanded the meaning of the phrase. To declare, "I wash my hands of it," apropos of whatever, means quite simply, "I don't give a damn." And the tagged-on simile, "like Pilate," is nothing more than a secular linguistic habit, a sort of muffled noise analogous to the thud a hefty body would make, falling into a pit.

One further comment: the Commonplace I'm trying (hopelessly) to elucidate here would be—rigorously and *in the Absolute sense*—equivalent to Cain's reply to God, "Am I my brother's keeper?" How true it is: bald though he may be, the Bourgeois can't spit out a single word without shaking the temple columns—like Samson!

But this is where I lose my wits. Didn't I just refer to the Absolute, forgetting that nothing is absolute, which I've already tied myself in knots to demonstrate? The truth is, I'm starting to fear I may never reach the end of this immense labor of exegesis, so much does the material overwhelm me, so much does the subject jumble my brain.

Post-scriptum. I've noticed that this Commonplace is ordinarily and inexplicably invoked by individuals with dirty hands—exactly like the mysterious Panthéon-Courcelles omnibus, which always stops in front of the bordello on the Rue des Quatre-Vents without anyone getting on or off, and without anyone being able to figure out why.

XXIII

PREACHING IN THE DESERT (LIKE ST. JOHN)

Prêcher dans le desert comme Saint Jean

The Gospel again! One could write quite a monograph on all the evangelical residue that turns up in the Bourgeois gut. The difficulty here is not insignificant, and once again I'm complaining about it.

My God! Of course I know what they mean—this professor of mathematics, this fellow hocking chestnuts, this member of the Académie Française—François Coppée, if you like, or Hanotaux[1]—I know what they mean when they claim that somebody is preaching in the desert... like Saint John. Yes, admittedly, I know what they *mean*, a child of three would know what they mean. But what I don't know is what they're really saying. It escapes me almost as completely as it does them.

Peculiar situation! How, for example, would such judges parse the word "preach"? And what do they understand by "desert"? As for Saint John, let's do everyone a favor and leave him out of it. When I read in the Gospel that "John the Baptist preached in the desert of Judea," all I have to do is continue along in the chapter in order to learn immediately that an enormous crowd of people came from all over to listen to him in this desert, that a great number of these had themselves baptized by him and became his disciples, and that, consequently, he was *not* preaching in vain. And yet François Coppée, and every other member of the aforementioned Académie Bourgeoise, appears to have reached the exact opposite interpretation.

So what do we make of this? Since it couldn't possibly be a matter of pure and simple asininity—that would be unthinkable!—doesn't this apparent confusion of the dative and ablative cases seem to conceal some incredible secret? Did these fellows receive some extraordinary revelation of I don't know what, invalidating the Sacred Text? I confess, the thought fills me with dread, and, from the very bottom of my despicable writer's heart, with all the humility a poor artist can muster, I thank the Lord for sparing me the so burdensome glory—of being born bourgeois.

---

1. François Coppée (1842–1908) and Gabriel Hanotaux (1853–1944) are recurring figures in Bloy's Exégèse. The former was a poet and novelist, one of the many literary friends with whom Bloy broke over the years. Hanotaux, a statesman and historian, was another close friend whom Bloy would later reject.

XXIV

HAVE YOUR HEAD IN THE CLOUDS

Être dans les nuages.

To love something other than what is ignoble, foul-smelling, and stupid; to covet Beauty, Splendor, Bliss; to prefer a work of art to a bit of filth and Michelangelo's *Last Judgment* to an end-of-the-year inventory; to need more urgently the satisfaction of your soul than the filling up of your intestines; to believe, finally, in Poetry, Heroism, and Holiness: this is what the Bourgeois calls "having your head in the clouds." From which it follows that the clouds are a kind of omnibus serving the homeland of whoever isn't located precisely at the bottom-most rung of the ladder—and, naturally, no one is. For there is a never-ending hierarchy of clouds, and the Adversary carefully hides this fact from mankind.

The proof is as simple as it is important. A poor journeyman sewage worker scraping the crust at the bottom of a ditch and dreaming of apple orchards or flowering acacias, has his head incontestably in the clouds. A commercial worker interrupting his invoices to devour the next installment of a Richebourg[1] serial, from which he gets a panting literary thrill, has his head even more in the clouds, if that's possible, and he already knows it himself. A notary, drunk with love, who plants a fourth child in his notaress, forgetting that he's already produced a hydrocephaloid and two sickly runts, has his head as deep in the clouds as possible, no question about it, and only something like the monstrosity of a pharmacist writing poems would be disturbing enough to top it. I could go on like this forever, to tell the whole truth.

To sum up, in order to take off instantly into the clouds, you have only to do, think, want or dream of something decent or quasi-decent, doesn't matter what, half a second is all it takes.

And so these famous clouds, which the Bourgeois so energetically reviles, await him—alas!—at every turn. Try as he might, he will never be sure to avoid them altogether, and this is why his fate—and fools everywhere are envious of it—turns out to be so painful! People have often wondered how the Bourgeois

---

1. Émile Richebourg (1833–1898) was a popular and prolific French novelist, most well-known for his serials appearing in Le Petit Journal.

could be such a pig, so villainously low, so sunk in muck, but really there's no mystery. Blame the clouds!

A loan shark had just croaked his last. His family begged Saint Anthony of Padua to give the funeral mass. He agreed, and his sermon, one hundred percent in the clouds, was on Matthew 6:21, "For where thy treasure is, there is thy heart also." The sermon finished, he turned to the dead man's relatives.

"Go now," he told them, "and look through the coffers of this fellow who's just died. You know what you'll find among those pieces of gold and silver? I'm going to tell you: you'll find his *heart*."

They went and they looked, and there indeed, among all that clanking money, they found a human heart, still warm and beating... Here was one, perhaps, who escaped the clouds.

How obnoxious the Ascension must appear to the Bourgeois! How it must revolt him, the idea of Jesus mounting up into the sky—a God in the clouds! And yet, can anyone point to a better Christian than this same Bourgeois? You can find him heading up all our parish charities, and he even handles the Transfiguration, clever boy!

XXV

DO AS YOU SHOULD

Être comme il faut.

No exception to this rule. Men to whom it doesn't apply will never do as they should. Therefore all superior people are excluded, eliminated immediately and without any preferential treatment. A man who does as he should ought to be, first and foremost, a man who does what every other man does. The more like everybody else you are, the more you're doing as you should. It's consecration by Multitude.

Dress as you should, speak as you should, eat as you should, walk as you should, live as you should, I've heard this all my life.

I wonder if you'll recall at this point what I said at the beginning of my exegesis, namely that in the form of Commonplaces the Bourgeois continually and unwittingly advances truly impressive claims, the implications of which are unknown to him but which would cause him to die of fright if he could actually hear himself.

Likewise, and with singular energy, the Commonplace under present consideration expresses the evangelical mandate of absolute Unity: *Sint unum sicut et nos.*[1] The substance of the Word being true in every sense, it is certain that, in his own way, the Bourgeois fulfills the Will he is ignorant of by insisting that the mass of humanity is an immense and uniform herd of imbeciles—to be sacrificed in atonement… one of these days.

---

1. John 17:11, "[That] they may be one, as we also are."

XXVI

BE PRACTICAL

Être pratique.

If you only ever consulted the dictionary, you might well believe this were simply a question of one thing and its opposite, which we would have to call *theoretical*, and which would not be any less worthy for that.

From this point of view, a practical man would be an instrument for the realization of an idea or the application of a law. The practical man *par excellence* would be the executioner. But that isn't what's at issue here.

In the Bourgeois idiom—a very particular idiom for which it is all too easy to express inadequate admiration—practicality is a whole collection of moral qualities, a state of the soul. One says of a man that he is practical in the same way one would say that he is virtuous, and even with a slight hint of disdain for virtue.

The practical man is in fact the true bourgeois demi-god, the modern substitute for the Saints of old. The larger part of contemporary statues have been erected in honour of practical men by other practical men, ever-so-sensible and always up at the crack of dawn.

A landlord who, in the dead of winter, forces the sick and starving onto the streets, is absolutely a practical man, even more so if he's a millionaire—and the more millions he acquires, the more practical he becomes. What raises this man up so high, is the fact that he has a heart, often even quite a tender one, and he knows how to suppress it with great generosity. There are those who make a living—and it's a pretty tidy living—supplying hospitals with cadavers or selling milk that poisons on average fifteen hundred children a year, and you know what? Every single one of these people is overflowing with love. But they're slaves to the principle: you have to be practical.

Another rule with no exception: a saintly man is never a practical one.

XXVII

MOUNTED FIRMLY UPON ONE'S PRINCIPLES

Être à cheval sur les principes.

A kind of horsemanship reserved exclusively for the Bourgeois—and it's by far the safest way to ride. Indeed, no one's ever heard of such a rider being unsaddled. But also: how admirably broken in, these principles! A mount all the more obliging given that it costs nothing and—look!—it just found the Cossack all by itself.

The bicycle and automobile are left in the dust, for Bourgeois horse-principles go even faster, and do a better job of crushing, and in a more satisfying, more irremediable way. Yes, they grind up the bodies of the weak and the innocent, who have no one to defend them—but not only their bodies! They also and especially grind up their souls.

The Bourgeois gallops forth on matchless principles, chargers of death that cannot be outrun, and which he lodges in the stable of his heart.

XXVIII

A POET IN HIS SPARE TIME

Être poète à ses heures.

I challenge you to find a Bourgeois who isn't a poet in his spare time. They all are, every last one without exception. The Bourgeois who isn't a poet in his spare time would be an affront to the wider fraternity and should be sent back in disgrace to the community of artists, that pack of slaves who are poets on someone else's time.

For example, it's a bit difficult to understand and explain what the Bourgeois' *spare time* poetry might really be. Suppose for a moment that this officer of the court is taking a break from the strain of his government job to tickle the muse (so to speak), that having produced so few writs and distraints he consoles himself by executing cantatas or elegies instead—this would obviously be to make a mockery of someone who deserves respect. The very idea of it, I daresay, is base.

The Bourgeois isn't an imbecile, nor is he a hooligan, and it's widely known that true poets—those who are only poets, who are poets at *all* hours and not only in their spare time—must be counted both imbeciles and hooligans. The Bourgeois, on the other hand, is a poet in such a way as befits a serious man, that is to say *when it pleases him* and *as it pleases him*, and without the slightest care one way or the other. He doesn't really even need to touch it—that's what servants are for. No need for him to read or to have read or even to be vaguely informed about this or that. All this man has to do is *exude*. The immensity of his soul splits open the heavens.

But there's a time for that, spare time, time when he's digesting a meal, for example. When it's time for business—when, that is, it's time to get serious—such jackassery is immediately set aside.

"To be a poet in one's spare time, and only in one's spare time, therein lies the secret of great nations." So it was said to me, in my childhood, by a member of the grand old bourgeoisie.

XXIX

IN AN INTERESTING SITUATION

Être dans une situation intéressante.

This one is exclusively for the ladies. A gentleman, even a bourgeois gentleman, will never find himself in an interesting situation.

What should we make of this phrase? If I see a pregnant bourgeois woman, it's impossible for me not to think of the impending birth of a—ahem—*petit bourgeois*, and I confess I find this rather troubling. I don't even quite see how the family could be concerned here, except in the most unfortunate sense. For, when it comes down to it, the Bourgeois is no patriarch, nor should he be one. Patriarchal virtues are precisely the opposite of those he prides himself on. He has no use for a vast posterity, and it's not as though he pictures himself leading a caravan through the solitary wastelands, worshipping Jehovah. Even when he procreates, the Bourgeois is taking care of business. Therefore what's under discussion here could only be some *interest* or other, at such and such a percent. That's the most we can say.

But these reflections don't shed much light on the subject. The polite formulation, "in an interesting situation," appears to be one of these commonplaces that doesn't make much sense and which only needs to be pointed out in passing, like something fearsome and probably dangerous that mustn't be gone into too deeply.

XXX

KEEP PACE WITH THE TIMES

Il faut être de son siècle.

Monsieur Culot had invented something, no one knew what, and he never took anyone into his confidence. He only wanted people to know that he wasn't an idiot and that, outside of his professional responsibilities—brilliantly performed, by the way—in his capacity as head accountant for the department of Sulfurs, he was what you might call *somebody*.

No one was better informed than he about every step in the progress of science. Since he subscribed to every journal and scientific bulletin and devoured them all, or pretended to devour them, people would consult him like a reference.

"You have to keep pace with the times," he would say, at every opportunity, judging his own times (which happened to be the nineteenth century) to be the absolute culmination of everything to which one could possibly desire to belong, so much so it made a person itch to be reborn in the most obsolete primordial dust. He refused to admit even the faintest supposition of defect or waste, and other centuries seemed to him, by comparison, altogether unbreathable.

He became an inventor in order to belong more fully to a time of inventions. But, I repeat, no one knew what to make of his discoveries. At his house there was a mysterious door always kept closed with three separate locks and upon which was written one simple word: LABORATORY—and the rumors went racing along.

Certain insinuations accompanied by vague smiles gave one to think he'd mastered the stratosphere and solved the problem of aerial navigation. Some presumed weightily that he must have rediscovered Greek fire or even black powder. One clever fellow, who slept with Madame Culot every Saturday, made whispers that he was the inventor of a barking machine that was destined to replace guard dogs in the city and the countryside. In short, no one knew what went on in there and no one ever would. But Monsieur Culot enjoyed great notoriety, and it was even expected he would land a post at the Institute, which certainly would have happened if not for the conspiracies.

And now we come to the bizarre denouement of his destiny, if it's possible, that is, to call this a denouement. The man had a godless, not especially beautiful, but perfect bitch of a daughter, who, no less energetically than he, wanted to keep pace with the times—though she paid not the slightest attention to her father's assiduous little machinations. Encouraged, I might add, by the example of her mother, who would have had people talking about her no matter the epoch, she'd obtained the most remarkable results very early in life.

By the time she turned eighteen—and in this respect she was quite different from her father—there wasn't anyone who *didn't* know the ins and outs of Mademoiselle Barbe Culot. At twenty-five, she had already gotten rid of several children—scientifically—which, when the circumstances were divulged, earned her (having by then become a first-class midwife) the congratulations of the President of the Republic and a medal of honor—this on the very day that Ricord's[1] statue was inaugurated.

But, says another Commonplace, there are two sides to every coin (which, numismatist that I am, I will study as soon as possible, when the time is right).[2]

One day, two men who kept pace with the times met as though by chance in the bedroom of this darling child who was, for the moment, naked as the day she was born and completely drunk. There was raised then such a clamor, I have no idea why, that Monsieur Culot could not refrain from rushing in and inviting these gentlemen to moderate their behavior.

"It's plain to see you aren't keeping pace with the times!" they answered.

The enormity of this remonstrance froze the old man in his tracks for several instants before he managed, finally, to stammer forth his apologies. He even went so far as to offer everyone refreshments, and calm was restored to the dwelling. But the blow had already been struck. Monsieur Culot, suspected of not keeping pace with the times, lost the color in his cheeks, fell into a doldrums, and ended up taking to bed. Feeling his demise was upon him, he asked to be cremated at public expense and gently expired, having called those present to bear witness that he had perished a man of his times. The community of scholars lamented the passing of this Archimedes.

---

1. The French doctor Philippe Ricord (1800–1899) was world-renowned for his treatment of venereal diseases, and a statue was indeed erected in his honor on the Boulevard de Port-Royal in Paris. —J. P.

2. Bloy never did get around to elucidating this commonplace. —J. P.

Nolite conformari huic sæculo—Be not conformed to this world![3] shouted Saint Paul, whose triumph was too easy and who surely would have understood nothing of the impenetrable wisdom of the Bourgeois.

---

[3]. Romans 12:2.

XXXI

MORE CATHOLIC THAN THE POPE

Il ne faut pas être plus catholique que le Pape.

At first glance, you might think the Pope would be happy there are people more Catholic than he, human alarm signals telling him to *Stop right there* when he goes too far—which is to say, all the time, *n'est-ce pas?* For the Pope is the only man who makes infallible mistakes, and in fact that's how the doctrine of Papal Infallibility ought to be interpreted. That's the Bourgeois interpretation, anyway.

Why does the Bourgeois complain then, when he comes across someone more Catholic than the Pope? Probably because the Pope is already too Catholic. Okay, I'm listening, but it's still not entirely clear.

If the Pope is always mistaken, and if, in his infallibility, he's the *only one* who's always mistaken, it follows that it's impossible *not* to be more Catholic than he. At the same time, O Bourgeois, you tell me that this is no good, that one *shouldn't* be more Catholic, which necessarily implies that one should be *less*, which, as has just been demonstrated, is impossible.

On this absurd supposition, the Pope is restored to his proper rank, as the sea to its "marvelous swellings,"[1] and here I am back on a level of Catholicism inferior to that of the Sovereign Pontiff, who cannot *not* be mistaken and who for this reason straightaway falls once again, invincibly, to the lowest rung. Once more, I ask for a little enlightenment.

---

1. Probably a reference to Saint Hilary of Poitiers' *The Trinity*.

XXXII

ALL TASTES ARE FOUND IN NATURE

Tous les goûts sont dans la nature.

In bourgeois nature anyway, but that goes without saying. Try to imagine such a universality of taste in a poet! And note, I pray you, we're not talking about a great variety or a great multiplicity of tastes here, we're talking about *all* tastes, from a taste for ambrosia up to and including a taste for shit.

But there's the Bourgeois for you, he loves everything and swallows everything. At least, clever fellow that he is, he'd have you believe so. But I know his inclinations, and I don't see him caring much for cleaner things. Therein lies his indisputable and sempiternal superiority, which, try though he might, he cannot hide.

XXXIII

SOME TRUTHS ARE BETTER LEFT UNSPOKEN

Toutes les vérités ne sont pas bonnes à dire.

And others, an even greater number, are just as well left unheard. So one must choose between this one and that, which supposes a level of discernment proper only to the angels—and what angels!

A truth that would expose whoever reveals it (or whoever witnesses the revelation) to some form of disgrace would, obviously, be better left unspoken. Live to fight another day, to each his own—your average Bourgeois is no martyr. But he isn't a confessor either, or a penitent starving for humiliation, and he prefers in his good judgment to ignore anything disagreeable to him—however true.

Which is all well and good, but here's something strange. If we were to eliminate in one fell swoop all the dangerous-to-speak truths and all the unpleasant-to-hear truths, what would we be left with? Because, search as I might, I've yet to discover a third category.

You know, let's just proclaim it without equivocation: *All truths are better left unspoken*, that's the text's real meaning. And maybe there isn't even such a thing as Truth. Pilate himself wasn't convinced, and he stared that TRUTH directly in the Face.

XXXIV

LOOKING FOR TROUBLE
WHERE NONE'S TO BE FOUND[1]

Chercher midi à quatorze heures.

They'll never fail to reproach me for this. They'll say I go looking for the Bourgeois where he isn't to be found, that I impute to him intentions, feelings, and ideas that he doesn't have. They'll say this and, well, they'll be wrong. I do not *go looking*, and I do not *impute*. The Bourgeois may be encountered at any hour of the day—clockmakers know this all too well—and he is capable of anything, as the poor have learned at their own expense. All I've said—and the present work has no other purpose—is that the Bourgeois is a senseless (but faithful) reverberation, echoing the Word of God when it rings out here in the world below. He is a dark glass reflecting fully the *mirror-image* of this same God's Face when He gazes down upon mortal waters. I added that, to me, there was something terrible in this. And that is all.

As for this wretched platitude, this fetid old refrain whose dismal banality filled my tormented childhood and which doesn't even have the diabolical excuse of *pretending* to imitate a sacred Text, I don't know what should be made of it.

It's similar to the *Nothing is absolute* from the first pages of this book. When a poor schoolboy pants with joy because he has found something, or believes he has found something, he is invariably dealt this cudgel blow of having complicated things unnecessarily.

I've already said it, and no doubt I'll be forced to say it again: preferring what is noble to what is ignoble and what is beautiful to what is hideous; seeking to understand, attempting to conquer whatever it may be by leaping over boundaries and limits; wanting to *live*, finally: this is what is anathema to them.

I'm trying to picture this appeals court litigator, having reached the expiration of a sordid life, dying at noon on the dot, and his filthy, weightless

---

1. Bloy's allusions to time of day in this passage resonate with the French *chercher midi à quatorze heures* (literally, "to look for noon at two o'clock"), which for metaphorical purposes has no English equivalent. I have taken a certain degree of poetic license throughout in order to approximate the effect.

soul dragged by the sobs of all the poor people he's crushed all the way to the Fourteenth station of the Cross,[2] which is the final bloody stage in the Trial and Passion of Jesus Christ!

---

2. In French, *la station de Quatorze heures,* i.e. two o'clock.

XXXV

CERTAIN LIMITS MUST NOT BE CROSSED

Il y a des bornes qu'il ne faut pas franchir.

This is a much cleaner formulation. You are informed that at a certain, not too great distance from here, there is a border whose transgression is unforgivable. Unfortunately you have to have good eyes to make it out, for it's rather difficult to see. On top of that, there is the complicating factor of its being unstable. It's a slack cordon that offers no exact definitions. Sometimes, the Bourgeois himself goes running past these limits without knowing it, and thereby falls prey, dishonorably, to the very trap he's laid for the Poets, mischievously assuming them to be moles.

Well, too bad for him. As for me, I'd welcome a revolution—let the the intolerable tyranny of the old Bourgeois, enemy of all adventure, be stood up against the modern frenzies of a reckless Bourgeois who wants to do away with limits altogether. The resulting cataclysm would spread a bit of harmony around our planet.

XXXVI

TOO MUCH OF A GOOD THING...

L'excès en tout est un défaut.

It's even possible to be *too* bourgeois, which seems paradoxical. Here, to give you the proof, is an extremely simple story from my childhood, in which I played a disreputable part.

Monsieur Robert, who drew a small private income from oil investments, was unhappy. Yet he shouldn't have been. The efforts of an entire career of commercial underhandedness had in his case been repaid with egalitarian opulence. Sometimes fate is just.

A house on the main boulevard stripped—thank heavens!—of all architectural profile attested to the financial importance of this prize-winning man. The inexorable whiteness of the roughcast inflamed one's eyes and killed off the surrounding vegetation.

By the carriage entrance you could make out a scorched, boiled, grim-looking garden, from which its owner's taste had banished all nature. Everything in it was gravel and ornamental plumbing. An impish cupid done in faux bronze contained a dribbling fountain in the middle of a little pool designed by the same Cyclops, in which a school of luckless goldfish seemed to be sweating.

A few hydrophobic geraniums were clustered here and there at the foot of some linden trees that had given up any pretense of freshness. You could also see multi-colored spherical mirrors, an old lawn game painted a washed-out asparagus green, a bower of Virginia creeper and completely sun-roasted wisteria, which only someone being burned alive would think to beg shade from. Last but not least the azure-colored kennel of a dog who had reached the last stage of scabious alopecia, but who was no less committed for that to surveilling the landscape. A prison wall crenelated with bottle glass blocked off the horizon. This charming abode was the glory of Monsieur Robert.

More lofty reasons summoned in him a perfect joy. He was a member of the City Council, was highly esteemed for the abundance and fluidity of his views, was called—people said—by a clamorous public, to more august employment. In a surfeit of happiness, his wife had died, and from then on awaited him in heaven, after having, over the space of thirty years, cuckolded him on earth.

Why did it have to be so? Why had the innards of this beautiful fruit to be gnawed by an unforgiving worm? Monsieur Robert had a neighbor who was poisoning his life and reducing him to despair. The contaminant was an engraver, a concupiscent slob of a man, whom he never encountered without shuddering and whose mere presence drove him mad.

This engraver, always slovenly-looking, always wearing a sort of Turkish fig basket for a hat, always puffing at the tip of some reed, would, in addition to his chiseling, engage in certain photographic practices of the least innocent kind, to judge by his usual confederates: a fat, extremely stocky assistant no landlord would want to encounter in a dark alley on rent-day, and a gloomy beanpole of a cameraman with silver nitrate eyes, knotted like a vine stock, who beneath the black hood of his apparatus resembled nothing so much as a masked executioner.

"None of this," Monsieur Robert would say, "was especially Catholic."

Women—wantons, probably—came most every day, to perform what offices God only knows! And there was no way *not* to see them, for Monsieur Robert wasn't entirely shut away behind his walls, and his garden was separated from the engraver's by no more than a simple openwork fence, which hid nothing.

How many times must his young daughter, a peevish, sentimental goat of a girl, have glimpsed in passing some orgiastic scene, the memory of which no doubt haunted her! I daresay she had seen these odious neighbors, male and female, shamelessly baring their breasts under the pretext of art, drinking aperitifs *al fresco* and groaning like animals. Which became all the more intolerable since they seemed to be mocking father and daughter, exploding with laughter whenever one or the other showed up.

One day, the abominable photographer had the audacity to turn his lens on them, presenting them the next day with the two portraits, accompanied by a fervent request that Mademoiselle Armandine be sent over for some more *comprehensive* studies. This unspeakable message, which Armandine unfortunately read, contained hypotheticals of inconceivable indecency... and the worst of it was that the ex-oilman's lawyer, whom he consulted immediately and knew for a serious man, had merely shrugged his shoulders and, with a great guffaw, advised him to leave the matter alone and lend no importance to such an obvious prank.

Well, as it turned out, the engraver with the fig-basket hat had become so insolent as to start addressing Monsieur Robert—who had always been a credit to his name, who had always paid his bills promptly and in full—using the familiar *tu* form! And he would even pat poor Monsieur Robert on the belly in the middle of the street, calling him *My favorite old rascal*. The dignified fellow could no longer sleep, drowning in this torrent of tribulations.

So: the engraver was Monsieur Robert's waking nightmare, and he would have done anything to be delivered from it. Suffice it to say, he kept an attentive eye on the man, hoping one day to uncover some manner of criminal chicanery. Supposing the fellow really was, as he boasted, making engravings in his hideaway, that so-called art may well have served to conceal horrible machinations. Because the fact is, you'll never get an honest man to believe you could need so many companions—males and females!—so many comings and goings, so much funny business, just to put some scratches on a copper plate. Something else must have been going on.

One fine morning, his doubts were confirmed. As he slipped toward the door, stepping lightly, as had been his custom since he began "keeping watch over the store," the all too familiar voice of his mysterious neighbor could be heard through the wall against which he had been obliged to press himself in his anxiety, and the following words, full of terror, quite distinctly reached his ears: "The cadaver is turning white."

Other words were pronounced which he couldn't make out, but these were more than enough and he knew what it was up to him to do. Nevertheless his legs buckled; he felt a deep chill, as though he himself were the cadaver, and, over the course of several minutes, had to mop his brow and try to buck himself up. So there had been no mistake after all! The neighbor really was a prize bastard, a villain of the most dangerous type, from which earthly justice would deliver him. Thanking Providence for the first time in his life, he rushed toward the police station.

Having been informed of the slaughter, the sergeant came running straightaway with three men. They entered the engraver's residence unceremoniously, despite the goggling eyes of his assistant whom they already had by the collar…

"Where's your boss?" demanded this minion of the law, gruffly.

"Huh? What's the problem? He's in the darkroom. He'll be out in two minutes. What do you want with him? You don't think we robbed somebody or something, do you?"

"Shut your trap!" said the sergeant. "You can tell it to the judge. Now open this door."

"To hell with this," replied the man. "I'm not gonna screw things up with my boss to entertain you guys. You want to talk to him, talk to him yourself, if you're in such a hurry. You'll see what he has to say to you."

The officer, drawing his weapon, advanced toward the terrible place.

"Oh, come on now," shouted the invisible character, "can't you jerks stop bothering me? What's all this racket about? I'm telling you the cadaver's going to be superb."

That was too much. The justice-loving soldier threatened to break the door down. Sure enough, it had to be done, and a confused Monsieur Robert saw his executioner come forth from the shadows, wearing his fig-basket hat, pipe at his bill, carrying in his fingertips the photographic print of a famous painting representing the death of Caesar or some other tyrant.

XXXVII

HOWL WITH THE WOLVES

Il faut hurler avec les loups.

Precious maxim that must have been inherited from some old dog. Howling—it goes without saying—is a litotes, a euphemism. The point is to do what wolves do, in other words, eat sheep, beginning (naturally) with those whom it is one's duty to look after.

The bourgeois clergy is unanimous in recognizing this as quite an agreeable pastime, mutton flesh being exquisite and good for the bowels of all breeds of dog. There's an ominous chapter in the Book of Ezekiel which seems to predict certain indigestions, but among the bourgeois clergy hardly anyone reads Ezekiel, and especially not in the diocese of Meaux, where I imagine it must be considered a bit *rococo*. I single out Meaux because I live there—rather poorly, in fact, being neither shepherd nor sheep dog—and because I've had occasion here to observe a few clerics that Bossuet failed to anticipate and who don't look much like *eaglets*.[1]

I'll have more to say about these servants of God later, and can promise you a certain luxuriousness of detail. In the meantime, I offer them the altogether ecclesiastical apologue of the guard dog who turned "barkless" from howling too much with the wolves, and who every morning gulped down the Flesh and Blood of the Lamb—in silence.

---

1. The implication being that these clerics little resemble their renowned predecessor, Jacques-Bénigne Bossuet (1627–1704), also known as "The Eagle of Meaux."

XXXVIII

ONLY THE TRUTH OFFENDS

Il n'y a que la Vérité qui offense.

Post-scriptum to number XXXIII. Almost forgot about this one. And didn't I tell you? Not only are some truths better left unspoken, but in his great profundity the Bourgeois assures us that the Truth alone gives offense.

Lies don't offend him, and never will. A lie is like the crazy uncle whose wealth the Bourgeois still hopes to inherit, whom he never gets tired of buttering up. When the Lie becomes manifest, which one day or another must come to pass, all it will have to say is, "Drop everything and follow me," and just like that it will be dragging along, not a dozen poor people, but millions of bourgeois men and women who will follow it anywhere it has a mind to go.

To date, the Truth alone has been made flesh, *Ego Veritas qui loquor tecum,*[1] and you know how rapturously it was welcomed. Indeed, no one mistook it for a minute: *Crucifigatur!* ONLY THE TRUTH OFFENDS!

Still, it's troubling to hear the Bourgeois saying such things, calm as can be, from dawn till dusk.

---

1. "I am Truth who speaks with thee."

XXXIX

AMBITION IS THE UNDOING OF MANY A GREAT MAN

C'est l'ambition qui perd les grands hommes.

But to figure out what the Bourgeois means by "a great man," that's not so simple. You might well think—anybody would—that to bourgeois eyes the greatest man is the one with the most money. A plausible opinion, sure, but *merely* plausible. There's more to the story than that.

Superior to the man who has a lot of money is another, fearsome man, who has the power to take money from other people and give them, in exchange, a few kicks in the ass. This, between the two, is incontrovertibly the greater man.

And yet there is a third, greater still, who is surely, if I may be so bold, the very greatest man of all: he who takes revenge on behalf of the Bourgeois for that offensive Truth we were just speaking about. Such a champion clearly has no need for riches or for spreading terror. He doesn't even need a great name like Renan or Voltaire. Were he no more than a bastard pedant, an inconsequential vagabond apostate dressed in verminous rags, he would yet be the Scipio Africanus of this enlightened Carthage that must be destroyed. That's enough. His ambition, if he had any, would be to share the glory of that immortal, iron-gloved soldier who, at matins on Good Friday, in the presence of the Pontifex Maximus, slapped the shackled Christ across the face.

But what then does this Commonplace want us to do with its disastrous "ambition"? I wonder. If there's one thing the Bourgeois essentially lacks, it's this same Greatness he so abhors. It won't therefore be *his* undoing, and my guess is this vexatious Commonplace was put into circulation by quite smallish men who wanted nonetheless to make an impression.

XL

YOU WEREN'T PUT ON THIS EARTH TO ENJOY YOURSELF

On n'est pas sur la terre pour s'amuser.

Sorry, but then would you mind telling me why we were put here, if not to enjoy ourselves? Are we here instead to suffer?

Yes and no, but let's make sure we understand one another. Bourgeois speech is double-edged, like the sword of Aod son of Gera, third Judge of Israel.[1] Suffering is for others; only the Bourgeois was put on this earth to enjoy himself. Forget this law and suddenly nothing makes sense.

It is written in the Gospel that the poor will always be among us. But of course. Does anyone expect the Bourgeois to bother himself with suffering? And it's not enough for him to have lackeys, he has to have slaves, poor wretches whose bodies he can wear out, whose souls he can cause to waste away. That's his enjoyment! Degrade their souls, defile them, drive them to despair... And when the poor man cries out in pain, he is offered this consolation: "You weren't put on this earth to enjoy yourself." He must believe himself among the damned.

---

1. Judges 3:15-16.

XLI

I'M NO SAINT

Je ne suis pas un saint.

The Bourgeois wouldn't dare say, "I'm no genius." So how is it he dares to say, "I'm no saint"? Both conditions should be equally odious to him, since they both belong to the order of the absolute. And yet plainly a whiff of holiness contains something more difficult for him to tolerate, something that nags more insistently at his sense of pride. Indeed, there's at least a chance a man of genius won't be an indisputable and irredeemable idiot. The same can't be said of saints—as everybody knows.

You must recall, however, that the language of the Bourgeois, which altogether excludes the Absolute, is swarming with surprises, with contradictions in terms, with nonsense and incoherencies and digressions, in the midst of which a foreigner would be dumbfounded, while the Bourgeois seems to get along quite well. For my part, trying as I am to throw a bit of light on this mess, I admit I often get lost in it and as a result of the investigation fall into a kind of coma that alarms my friends.

For example, how does one reconcile the desire—so obvious, so bourgeois, so reasonable—*not* to be a saint with the customary requirement that others, particularly inferior people, be saints themselves? For such is the gist of this Commonplace, quite analogous to the preceding. Sainthood is *for others*, just like suffering is.

But everything works itself out in the end. The Bourgeois doesn't want to be a saint, and shouldn't be a saint, and so it becomes necessary that others be saints *for him*, so that he might have some peace, so that he might belch and digest his meal in peace. It's religion for the serving class, as advocated by Voltaire, which consists in loading one's bundle on somebody else's back.

You'll notice I'm not talking about the rudimentary Bourgeois here, the monopetalous Bourgeois, if you'll forgive the term, who "has nothing against God *per se*" and only thinks with his belly. Special mention will be made, however, of the Sneering Cynic, who considers anyone who performs a religious act an *a priori* hypocrite and makes every effort to brand him with this suspicion.

In his famous *Travels in China*, Monsieur Huc[1] explains the extreme frequency of suicide among the Chinese. In other countries, if a man wishes to wreak his vengeance on an enemy, he tries to kill him; in China, on the contrary, he kills himself. By such means, he may be sure of getting [his enemy] into horrible trouble; for he falls then immediately into the hands of justice, and will certainly be tortured and ruined, if not deprived of life. The family of the suicide also usually obtains, in these cases, considerable damages; so that it is by no means a rare case for an unfortunate man, from a morbid sense of familial devotion, to commit suicide in the house of a rich one.[2]

This curious passage came to mind as I contemplated my bourgeois. From a strictly religious point of view, the refusal of or absence of desire for sainthood is no different from suicide, since in absolute terms and when all is said and done, there is no condition apart from the condition of being a saint that is not also the condition of being dead—truly dead, eternally dead, the death of someone who detests his own soul. Such dead people have killed themselves, likewise, with the intention of losing their brothers. The man who will *readily* say, "I'm no saint," has in spiritual terms performed the same frightful act as his desperate Chinese counterpart. He's in the dark, so thinks he's only hopping over a single step; in fact, he's straddling the abyss.

---

1. Évariste Régis Huc, aka L'abbé Huc (1813–1860), a French Catholic priest and missionary, famous for his travel accounts of Qing-era China and Tibet.

2. Adapted from the 1859 translation. See Huc, Evariste Régis, 1813–1860. *The Chinese Empire: a Sequel to "Recollections of a Journey Through Tartary And Thibet."* New edition. (London: Longman, Brown, Green, and Longmans, 1859), p. 290.

XLII

I DON'T CLAIM TO BE ANY BETTER THAN I AM

Je ne me fais pas meilleur que je ne suis.

Ha, ha, Bourgeois, enough joking around! You're no saint, after all—on that point I agree—and humility doesn't suit you. It's not a question of claiming to be better or worse, simply of being what you are. And you are very good, without deserving to be or trying to be, thanks only to the excellence of your nature. Any better and you'd be too good. Who knows, you might even donate your money to starving poets...

But let's put all that aside. In general, when the Bourgeois declares that he isn't claiming to be any better than he is, you can be sure he couldn't make himself look any *worse*, however much he might like to, and that even as he speaks he's cooking up something rotten.

"You dirty bastard!" howls a man condemned to death, addressing himself to the executioner who's getting ready to cut his hair.

"*I don't claim,*" says the headsman, in an oh-so-gentle voice, "*to be any better than I am.*"

XLIII

SPEECH IS SILVER, SILENCE IS GOLDEN

La parole est d'argent, le silence est d'or.

Here's one that will never be understood. The height of ridiculousness would be to hope for even a single person to listen when you say, for example, that in the depths of the sacred Book, Speech and Silver are synonyms, while all-golden Silence is an image of eternal Life.

Try warning someone how dangerous and perhaps unforgivable it is to meddle with temperamental Forms, like the genie in the German fable,[1] rushing with all his dreadful power to obey a foolhardy magician who can't figure out how to get rid of him. You might as well ask for a straitjacket.

I won't try to warn anybody, therefore, and will instead limit myself to saying, without hope of being heard, that this beloved silver, this money[2] that gives the Bourgeois his exclusive purpose in life, signifies—how shall I say it?—a mysterious Will, whose expansive energy is incalculable and which is, however, only the *currency* of the Unspeakable designated by this golden and eternally desirable Silence, to which the entire bourgeoisie is cordially invited, alas, in vain.

When the sleeping Lord of the Prophet-King rolls over on his bed of centuries, a supernatural transformation will occur, analogous to the one that ushered in the Christian Era. Jesus will effectively no longer be seen, the Word will seem to fade away, the formerly apostolic Preachments will cease, while at the opposite extremity of the sky there will appear the prodigious golden Face of He who calls Himself, inscrutably, Silence!

That's what the tax man in my district says, without even knowing it, as he lines his impregnable coffers with pilfered, jingling coins.

---

1. Goethe's *The Sorcerer's Apprentice.*
2. The word *argent* in French means both "silver" and, more generally, "money." Bloy exploits such double meanings throughout the *Exegesis.*

XLIV

I DESERVE TO TAKE IT EASY

J'ai bien gagné de me reposer.

Monsieur Widespread owns the place, and he knows it. He even knows the law is on his side. But he insists on ignoring his renters, his doctor having urged him to avoid such emotions as tend to accompany being shouted at. He suffers, it would appear, from the overdevelopment of his sympathetic nervous system.

To help him escape from complaints and recriminations, he employs a stout-hearted manager, a former court bailiff or notary clerk who knows all the ins and outs and whose palm he greases with such and such a percentage to keep everything running smoothly.

Anyway, this management business is no sinecure, as Monsieur Widespread has several buildings in his possession, almost all of them inhabited by laborers whose money, every Saturday, must be captured as it were *on the fly*. There are also to be found in these barracks a fair number of companionable young women with irregular incomes and changeable friendships. Rent-collection among these people is less a comfort than a peril.

"I'm the landlord who doesn't want to know anything," Monsieur Widespread was saying, after double-checking the sums one day. His manager had just come over with four teeth missing and a face that looked like a forest landscape in late October. *"I deserve to take it easy."*

Admirably put! He's been seen taking it easy for the past thirty years or so, ever since the felicitous death of his parents left him in possession of their considerable fortune—acquired, rumor has it, at the town limits, highwayman-style. A potential marriage in the prime of his life was roundly rejected by the then young man, who, from a very early age, had loved money with chaste devotion.

Having now become a practical man, all he sees in the passions, whether juvenile or senile, is the value they might yield the philosopher who knows how to turn them to his advantage. He has even, you might say, raised up from its ruins and gloriously restored an historic and hundred-year old brothel from the time of the last Capetians, whose productivity would be the privilege of a *Son of France*. It wasn't as though this work left him with an aching back, however, and, since he's always going on about his well-earned rest, we are confined to speculations about God knows what *anterior* exhaustions, such as defy human memory.

"This Widespread of yours," some sharp mind told me the other day, "is a ghost, plain and simple. What he refers to as rest is, in fact, death. Maybe you've heard of people who appear to be alive but who in reality are dead? That's what's going on with almost all these vampires that you call the bourgeoisie. They only appear to be standing, making gestures and so forth—in fact they're lying down completely still. You're convinced they're speaking or, if you like, uttering sounds, while the strict truth is they're on a lower frequency than silence itself, sunk in the thickest sludge of a most uncomfortable silence. In order to lay bare their indubitable putrefaction, their frightful stench, all that's needed is a *simple* word, spoken by a living person. Pay careful attention next time someone's telling you how they 'deserve to take it easy.' Believe me, you'll smell the rot."

My interlocutor was right. No more than a few days ago, I had to deal with one of these dead people, so afraid he might wake up he didn't even mention taking it easy. As soon as he opened his mouth, I had before and against me a volcano of putrescence, an Orinoco of sanies in which I thought I would drown.

XLV

MONEY CAN'T BUY HAPPINESS, BUT...

L'argent ne fait pas le bonheur, mais...

A first-rate Commonplace which calls for the archetypal confidant of Greek tragedy. Someone has to add right away: "But it sure can make a contribution." Well that's all lovely then.

This humble contribution, swooping in so fortuitously to temper the melancholy harshness of a confession that might otherwise be taken for blasphemy, must be singularly efficacious. It's like sugar for one's conscience or a balm for the heart.

"Yes, it's true," the Bourgeois muses profoundly, "money can't buy happiness, especially when you don't have any." It probably *almost* can, just not completely. Something's missing, as everyone is forced to acknowledge, and to witness money's impotence in this regard gives rise to an infinite sadness. Money, after all, was supposed to ensure the bliss of those who adore it, for it truly is a God.

I've pointed out on more than one occasion that this metal, significantly *depreciated* in our time, is, in the Holy Book, a figure very much associated with the suffering Word, which is the Second Person of the divine Trinity, the Redeemer. To say that it cannot procure our happiness is therefore, for every Christian, so audacious an affirmation as to be considered impious—and, let's remember, this is an Expression with Christian origins. The proof for me is in the toning down of such a beautiful style, which *taxes* God for contributions to the joy-fund of imbeciles.

A pagan wouldn't mince words: "Money buys happiness," he would say, and he would be horrifically right to say so. But you, degenerate Bourgeois so-called Christian, upon whom all symbols of divine Life dissolve, like pearls on a leper, into pus; you, who most certainly believe in the beatitude of the hundred dollar bill: why lie? What could you possibly have to fear? You have a fathomless inability to grasp the prophetic Assimilations, and it wouldn't occur to you to be afraid that, by constantly bringing up Money, you might summon the bloody Face of Christ!

XLVI

GET BACK IN THE MONEY[1]

Rentrer dans son argent.

In the wake of what's just been said, this one has something staggering to it. Indeed, what does it mean to "get back," if not to be newly returned to the thing or person you had previously left? You can get back into your house or your shell; you can get back into the barracks after serving your watch, which is rather tiresome; you can even get back out into the world, almost as soon as you've left it, even if you're supposed to be home sick, if once again you feel the need. Basically, you can get back into whatever you want, on the condition, however, that the necessary and reciprocal considerations obtaining between *what goes in* and *what may be gone into* are observed.

Metaphorically, I can also understand a person "getting things back to normal," "getting back to the subject at hand," "getting back to his usual self," etc., since we're continuing to posit some enveloping thing that permits both exodus and reintegration. In a pinch I could even allow for a return to nothingness, which doesn't seem easy.

But to "get back in the money" is beyond my comprehension. You would have to imagine, which would be insane, something like a river or an ocean of money in which, at a certain time of year, you could bathe yourself. The "money season," you might call it, the way people say it's high season at Trouville or Evian. And in that case you could just as easily get into other people's money as your own. Yet it appears this is neither said nor done.

Why?

---

1. This one presents several difficulties. In colloquial usage, *rentrer dans son argent* means "to recoup one's expenses," but since Bloy plays with *rentrer* in its primary and literal sense ("to return" or "to go back into"), the straightforward English rendering won't hold when, later in the text, he explores its metaphorical possibilities. What's more, the English expression is transitive where the French is intransitive, undermining otherwise serviceable analogs. "Get back in the money" splits some of these differences but necessarily sacrifices integral elements of the original (e.g. the possessive in *son argent*).

XLVII

EVERYONE HAS TO LIVE

Il faut que tout le monde vive.

It would be puerile to ask the Bourgeois what he means by the words "to live." The novelists he deigns to confide in, those of the naturalistic or psychological school, have sufficiently demonstrated that "living" consists in fulfilling all the digestive, soporific or generative functions attributed to the different animal species, but also and above all in earning lots of money—which is what demarcates human nature, essentially, separating it from that of other beasts. Long before these doctors came on the scene, it was generally acknowledged that a man who ate a hearty meal on a regular basis was a *bon vivant*.

Still, *everyone*? That's a bit much. Isn't it enough that the Bourgeois is living, the Bourgeois alone?

In the language of religion, very different from his own, *to live* has another meaning, as well he knows. But what concern is this anomaly to the Bourgeois? If nutjobs and hysterics want to gratify what they call their *souls* by choosing to starve to death, that's their business. But that they would look on *us*—we BOURGEOIS—as though we were carcasses in the last stages of decomposition, it's too funny by half. Know ye this, once and for all, you sanctimonious prigs and sacristans, we're more religious even than you, and the proof is that we couldn't give two shits about the Kingdom of Heaven or so-called Eternal Life!

XLVIII

ALL ROADS LEAD TO ROME

Tous les chemins mènent à Rome.

Invincible argument in favor of the theory that our planet is indeed round. Were there a road that didn't lead to Rome, I trust it would be the road of choice, for, in the end, Rome is the Pope, *n'est-ce pas?* Only there is no such road. All imaginable roads steer the traveler Rome-ward: impossible to escape that holy terminus.

As luck would have it, though, we're under no obligation to follow it all the way to the end. There's always the option of stopping at a fork and taking another road—which will also lead unfailingly to Rome, yes, but to Rome by way of the Society Islands or North Cape, which puts the danger at a certain remove. You could even and without much trouble spend your whole life traveling this way, criss-crossing the planet in circles around the stationary See.

Any furniture or architecture tourists who'd like to enjoy a bit of leisure with their spouses during the off-season: this advice is for you.

XLIX

PARIS WASN'T BUILT IN A DAY

Paris n'a pas été bâti en un jour.

I've heard the same thing said of Rome, and plausibly enough. I don't know how many days it took to build a city this large, but it's highly likely many several were required. What's more, it doesn't make the least bit of difference.

What does matter, with regard to our moral and philosophical study of the Bourgeois, is his desire, repeatedly expressed in this very form, for Paris *not* to have been built in a day. Something in the mere possibility of it gnaws at him. Surely the Bourgeois would be completely indifferent to such a fact, yes? But no! No, indeed. Had Paris been built in a single day, this man would be in a state of utter despair. For him it would amount to an almost unspeakable assault upon the Matter-of-Fact, the Bit-by-Bit… upon Platitude itself!!! In short, a kind of miracle!

The truth, however, must be spoken. Paris, such as it is today, with its million houses, obviously couldn't have been built in the space of twenty-four hours, especially if we take into consideration the statue of Gambetta or the Pont Alexandre III, which are the sort of masterpieces you don't just throw together.

But Paris, immense as it is, had its own little beginning. There was a moment when nothing existed at this particular point along the two banks of the Seine, and there was another moment, consecutive to the first, when something did exist, a thatched roof, some hut or other that was made to last. At that precise moment, we can and must say that Paris was—virtually, potentially, and therefore, yes, quite literally—built. I would add that it must have been much more beautiful then, incomparably, incommensurably, unimaginably more beautiful. But how to express this in such a way that anyone will understand?

L

RAIN AND SHINE

La pluie et le beau temps.

The science of meteorology must have been cooked up in a green grocer's. We all know the scrupulous exactitude with which these respectable merchants inform their every customer, every day, without exception, about the certain or merely probable state of the atmosphere. Nothing escapes them, nary a cloud, nor ray of sunlight, nor chill wind, nor zephyr, and everyone takes advantage of it on the spot.

What bowls me over is the diligence and indefatigability of these benevolent information providers. They would share what they know with a thousand shoppers, they would share it with the devil!

"What else can I get for you?" they say from behind a broad smile. Answer impatiently that you have everything you came for, bellow it at them, throw in a few rageful gestures for good measure. "Oh, well. Next time, then!" they'll sigh, no less full of love, and they'll walk you out and, when you reach the threshold, grace you with one last favorable (as favorable as possible) prognostication.

Rain and shine are our universal resources which never run out. "Our *conversation* is in heaven,"[1] said Saint Paul. Astonishingly prophetic words that may be verified, thirty million times a day, nineteen centuries later, not only at the grocery store, but wherever the bourgeois are found.

Not a few of them reach a grand old age, and die surrounded with respect, in the most advanced stages of senility, without ever having spoken of anything *other* than what happens in the sky above.

---

1. Philippians 3:20.

LI

THE MOST DECENT OF DECENT PEOPLE
La crème des honnêtes gens.

Édouard was seventy-five years old and Rosalie sixty-five, but their consciences so clean people thought they were younger. "They didn't owe anybody anything." They "had never done anyone wrong," and, therefore, "had nothing to be ashamed of." They were said to be *the most decent of decent people*—no less!—which quite simply exhausts the limits of human praise.

Like the Nile, Édouard concealed his true source. He confessed only to having served as a domestic at, and later as manager of, a residential hotel in an unspecified neighborhood at an unspecified time. What remained to him of this past was his breathless affability, an asthmatic cordiality, and that sort of hypocritical do-gooder whininess, moaning and rubbing his vertebrae, worn out with being so helpful and sacrificing himself for everyone else.

The habitual wink with which he would underline certain salacious remarks, whose refinement he wanted you to appreciate, was generally accompanied by an inexplicable frog-like swelling motion, from low to high, beneath the lateral part of the skin of his old face, and, together with all of this, a catarrhal burbling, to gave the irreproachable man's physiognomy its final touch. Did I mention he preferred to be addressed as *Monsieur* Édouard?

A generation ago Rosalie (that is, *Madame* Édouard) had been a chambermaid in the household of a marquise—yes, my dear, an honest-to-goodness marquise who came, alas, like all good things, to an end, leaving her maid a bunch of outfits in the latest Second Empire fashion, along with, I believe, a few crowns, which, in addition to the conscientious *skimmings* of a quarter century or so, had turned her into a presentable catch at the age of forty-five. For it was around this time that the lucky Édouard wed her, having managed to soften her heart with his clever ruminant's countenance.

Extremely oracular and full to bursting with the wisdom of nations, she made you think one of Henri IV's old trollops had somehow survived the monarchy. Another bit she picked up from the marquise was a stunning top to bottom pomposity—woe to anyone who took her for a member of the vulgar masses—and the four steps leading up to the entrance of the happy couple's home had plainly been crafted to highlight the ostentation of her magnificent posturing.

I wasn't able to learn whether Monsieur Édouard's former bachelor's quarters had been held by this same *grande dame* or whether that episode preceded their marriage. Assuming this was the case, however, her presence would have brought some first-rate flavor to the business, enlivening the monotonous comings-and-goings of chamber pots and salad bowls with aristocratic lyricism.

Nature-lovers both, they finally retired a short ways outside the city limits, on the dry and not especially Appian way of one of our suburban cemeteries. Having split an already tiny house four ways and huddling up together, flattening themselves down like bugs, they were able to accommodate renters and thus realize their lifelong dreams.

But a pyramid, alas, has its highest point, beyond which it is given no one to ascend any further. Once you reach the top, the only thing left to do is to come back down. Édouard and Rosalie had stumbled upon a lousy tenant...

As everyone knows, a lousy tenant is one who fails to come up with the rent precisely *once*, no matter whether he's paid up several hundred times before, no matter whether he's saved the Fatherland thirty or forty times over. Why, even your Latin Grammar implies that Aristides was a lousy tenant, no? After all, he died a pauper!

In short, for several years already, Monsieur Édouard had been renting the most important part of his house to a poet. Yes, you read that correctly: a *poet*. Only the landlord had been fooled in most odious fashion. This poet had called himself a *writer*, and, naturally, old Édouard, imbued—indeed, dripping—with respect, believed himself to be in the presence of a ledger clerk,[1] a copyist in some office or other. He *so* believed this, in fact, that even the sight of several books with this supposed calligrapher's name on the spine, even *having read* several news articles wherein the poor scrivener was called a nobody reprobate and a slimy halfwit—which is, however, the very stamp of genius—his eyes could not be opened to the truth!

Nothing less than the tenant's sudden and obvious poverty, and the likely impossibility of his being able to pay for the next term, could remove the scales from his eyes. It was a rough blow for Monsieur Édouard. The dignified

---

1. The landlord's mistake plays on *écrivain* (writer) and *écritures* (an accountant's entries)...

man set about scolding and chiding, and the worse things got for the tenant's wife, who was dangerously sick and in dire need of peace and quiet, the more vehemently the landlord went after her husband. By that time, probably, he wasn't owed anything further—that would have been the last straw—but while he may have been the most *helpful* of men, he wasn't about to let some poor bugger make an ass of him, etc. No choice but to dispose of this most decent but spoiled cream of the bourgeois crop, who had been transformed into a man possessed, squealing like a pig at slaughter, at the mere possibility of not being paid.

But listen to what happened, exactly as it happened, before my very eyes. The sick woman, overcome by this situation, fell into a frightful delirium, from which it was feared she might never recover. For several days and nights she saw this old man and his crone, butchering human beings and selling their flesh to restaurateurs or sausage-makers. It was a continual, relentless obsession, which they pursued with unheard of precision, intensity and determination. These landlords were spilling blood—*spiritually*—and we were spattered with it, to the point of nausea and bodily horror.

This sick woman was more lucid than a clairvoyant, and I later came to understand that what she had SEEN was really the past of these servants of the Devil, in the incommensurable photographic negative that envelops the universe. Only what she had witnessed, by an effect of transposition which I am unable to explain or qualify (though I cannot deny the devastating *fact* of it), was the objective manifestation of appalling thoughts and feelings *in their true form*.

SHE HAD SEEN THE WATER OF TEARS TRANSFORMED INTO BLOOD!

Fortunately, Édouard and Rosalie were able to get rid of their poet. They didn't lose a penny, and they even had the presence of mind to swipe a few odds and ends during the moving process. How could the heavens not shine upon them? They're on great terms with their parish priest, who holds them up as a shining example. And they don't owe anything to anyone, not even to the Three Divine Persons who are One in God!

LII

FAMILIAL HONOR

L'honneur des familles.

In times gone by, when the meaning of words had yet to be abolished, a family's honor consisted in producing for the world either Saints or Heroes or, at the very least, useful servants of the *res publica*. This whether you were rich or poor, whether you had illustrious ancestors or not. If the latter, you would simply and naturally climb the aristocratic ladder, following the natural order of things.

These days, by contrast, familial honor consists uniquely and exclusively in avoiding the police.

Enlightened members of the bourgeoisie will sometimes agree—having asked for a moment to think on it—that in a very small number of cases, which they are ever so careful not to specify, poverty *might not* amount to dishonor, but nothing would erase the shame of conviction in a court of law, especially in the provinces.

For centuries altars have been decorated with the bones of Martyrs, the Church has announced their feast days and showered them with glory—to what end? The Bourgeois, full of suspicion, sees them as bungling suckers who let themselves get pinched and now are stuck with a criminal record. If Saint Lawrence had a niece, she wouldn't find anyone to marry her, and if the Penitent Thief had a fourth cousin twice removed, he'd never be offered even a mediocre post in the civil service.

The revulsion in which the Bourgeois holds Christianity stems in large part from his sense of honor—a point that hasn't been given adequate attention. It's hard for him to come to terms with a religion whose "founder," having suffered a scandalous punishment, was then resurrected on the third day in order to *compound* his family's dishonor for all eternity.

LIII

WORLDLY OBLIGATIONS

Les devoirs du monde.

Ego non sum de hoc mundo.[1] I am not of this world. *Jesus Christ was not a* MAN OF THE WORLD. He said so himself. So there exist obligations apart from him and, therefore, opposed to him, which are called Worldly obligations.

You have to have seen it yourself to understand what merciful forbearance there is in the smile of a Bourgeois listening, for example, to some sermon espousing contempt for material wealth or admiration for Christian purity.

"All things considered," that good-natured smile seems to say, "I'd rather listen to this than go deaf." Meanwhile he dreams of his true obligations, which are to spit in the Savior's Face and crucify Him, every day, in the wake of an unspeakable Scourging.

---

1. John 8:23.

LIV

HABIT IS A SECOND NATURE

L'habitude est une seconde nature.

"...I've caught the plague! It's not impossible the plague should be a consequence of error or evildoing; you say so and I don't deny it. I'm on the road to death, that much is certain; I may be, possibly, on the road to hell, and this may all be the effect of some error. It's true that I'm getting bored, that age is dulling my sensations, that death will come. These are unpleasant thoughts.

"Nevertheless, were God to suggest that I might for one moment be free of these boring, monotone, mendacious, dying and deadly things, which drive me to my present despair no less than to my eternal despair, and if He then offered to exchange them for Life, Joy, and Beatitude, I would refuse, I wouldn't even listen to it. I would go play some game that bores me and say to Him, 'Away with you! Away, you master of ecstasy and proprietor of joy! Away! Away, you sun, who rises in streams of purple and gold! Away, majesty! Away, splendor! Away! Away, you, who sweated blood in the garden of Olives! Away, you, who were transfigured upon Mount Tabor! Away! I'm going to the café, where I'm always bored.'

"But why go there?"

"Because that's what I always do."[1]

---

1. The entire passage is quoted from Ernest Hello. See *L'homme* (Paris: Perrin et Cie, 1894), 32-33.

LV

MAKE YOURSELF COMFORTABLE

Où il y a de la gêne, il n'y a pas de plaisir.

One night, Forain[1] was on the receiving end of a vigorous flurry of blows, skillfully delivered by a pair of truncheon-wielding bodyguards in service to some offended princess of Pigalle. The beloved caricaturist of oafs and boors confessed to not having taken any pleasure[2] in this; indeed, the incident must have poisoned him for life, for I've been told that, ever since, the sight of a hard stick,[3] even attached to a tree, causes him a sharp sensation of discomfort.

Thinking of this Commonplace, it would have been hard for me not to recall Forain and his adventure, which may well have been repeated many times—this was ten years ago, after all.

But the example is worthless. It's not as though every bourgeois is subjected to regular thrashings, and there are plenty of commercial travelers and court bailiffs for whom Forain is a great artist. It serves my exegesis well enough to put forth the observation that this word *uncomfortable*, both in its primary sense of painful unease, as well as in the sense of financial shortfall, rules out any possibility of pleasure.

For example, the holy law of divorce obtained by a cuckold-in-the-making blessed with a Tartarian camel's hump came along at just the right moment to deliver the joyful French nation from the discomfort of insoluble bonds. It's true the effect ends there, and that divorcees don't receive any dowry when they remarry—an annoying oversight which will certainly be put right, one of these days, by some goitrous legislator.

No point mentioning shoes that are too narrow, or rib-crushing whalebone corsets, or tacks that might be sat upon, or any other peripeteia that might interfere with having a laugh. In every imaginable case, pleasure is required, at whatever price, and what is uncomfortable must forever and absolutely be barred, so says the Prince of this world, father of the Bourgeois, enemy of Redemption through Sacrifice.

---

1. Jean-Louis Forain (1852–1931), French painter and caricaturist. Bloy likely knew him through Barbey d'Aurevilly. —J. P.

2. Taken literally, the original French expression matches *pleasure* against *discomfort*.

3. The word *trique* (rod or cudgel) is also common slang for an erection, and Bloy clearly leans on that double-meaning here.

LVI

NO PLEASURE WITHOUT PAIN

Il n'y a pas de plaisir sans peine.

Without pain for *other people,* of course. It would be a bit excessive, forcing the Bourgeois to pick up the tab for some pleasure or other at the cost of his own personal displeasure. On close consideration, it's identical to the Commonplace that precedes it. Another one young people use when they want to express themselves in a manner both poetic and original, is "Every rose has its thorn"—which does not at all mean they've resigned themselves to the pricks they might sustain while innocently harvesting the queen of flowers.

Neither male nor female Bourgeois can be understood until this idea has sunk in: that because today they are masters of the world, whatever pain there is to suffer is to be suffered by their slaves—that is, anyone and everyone who is not, like them, bourgeois. And yet, among these more or less innumerable slaves, a portion are in fact volunteers. There are, if you will, the Carmelites and the Benedictines, daughters flung sometimes from the highest peaks of the aristocracy, who have freely chosen the most arduous life in order that the Bourgeois might have nothing to suffer *upon this earth,* in order that this frightful little spawn of Christ's Blood, who places no hope in another life, who does not want to place hope in another life, might at least enjoy the peace of brutes in this one.

He's aware of none of this, it goes without saying, and wouldn't understand it even if he was, even if some angel devoted a century to explaining it to him. Nevertheless, he has a kind of intuition about it, up to a certain point. A sort of animal sixth sense alerts him to the fact that others are working, taking pains on his behalf, and that a certain *justice* is thereby being executed which, one day, will have him screaming in terror…

When he says there's no pleasure without pain, it's rather like the stupefied and slightly panic-stricken irony of an incompetent soldier, acutely aware his comrades won't go marching to their deaths for him eternally.

LVII

YOU CAN'T MAKE AN OMELETTE WITHOUT BREAKING SOME EGGS

On ne fait pas d'omelettes sans casser des œufs.

Such were the terms by which the colossal Bourgeois Abdul-Hamid had to explain the massacre of two or three hundred thousand Armenian Christians to his good friend and loyal servant, Hanotaux.[1] Only he didn't offer him the omelette to eat.

Gabriel, sent away with a meager gratuity, did what he could to lick his wounds, having (I dare hope) scraped a few rings in the bottom of the Ministry of Foreign Affairs' pan, where—in the tradition of Richelieu—his passing fancies brought so much honor to France.

Having known this statesman quite well myself, I consider it infinitely likely his admiration for the sultan only increased. The son of a petty bourgeois family from Saint-Quentin, his bowels must have been more than stirred by this Padishah, a man possessing (on good authority) several tens of millions in private income and responsible for massacring the population of fifty cities!

When a bourgeois talks about breaking eggs to make an omelette, you can bet there will always be someone, or some many, standing by to take the blows full force—and a Hanotaux to clap hands in approval.

---

1. As French Minister of Foreign Affairs, Gabriel Hanotaux (see above note to XXIII) took the position that to admonish Turkey for the atrocities against its Armenian population would be commercially and strategically disadvantageous for France.

LVIII

I DON'T HAVE ANY CHANGE

Je n'ai pas de monnaie.

A wretched soul begs a hundred centimes, having already asked in vain for twenty francs, and this is the reply some bigshot sends shining back at him. It's not even a question of alms. The beggar is no stranger and promises to work off the debt. No—what am I saying?—he's already worked it off, but he doesn't have the means to bridge the gap from now till payday.

As misfortune would have it, the person being solicited is a man of "firm principles," who never lends money on credit. A hopeless case if ever there was one. Perform a miracle if you like, there's no overcoming this particular species of bourgeois. A cadaver's rigidity is less unyielding to Prayer than the rigidity of this man's principles.

That said, because the other fellow looks so desperate, because his insistence is so extreme, and since they happen to be in a more or less deserted place, the bourgeois temporarily refrains from talking about his principles and answers only that he doesn't have any change.

"Would you like me to make some for you?" says the other.

A terrifying proposition.

The Bourgeois thinks he's hearing the voice of a brigand threatening him with death. Nevertheless an idea comes to him. He declares his intention to make some himself at that well-lit intersection—you see it—just down there at the end of the avenue. Arriving there with his companion, he points the latter out to a pair of cops who immediately take him into custody.

Sure enough, the wretched soul will sleep at the station that night, and the poor little ones waiting for their dinner will have to grind their teeth and do without. There exist such frightful things as this. He who has never seen nor heard little children *grinding their teeth* has no knowledge of the depths of human suffering.

The just man, free at last and happy with himself, hails a cab and goes off to make change for himself in an all-night restaurant. So all is rather well. But here's another wrinkle. This very night, while he's out carousing, the giant construction sites he owns go up in flames, and tomorrow the newspapers will report the loss at six hundred thousand francs!

What to make of this? Could it be that certain words are combustible *in and of themselves*, without the intervention of any visible hand? The desperate man is under lock and key, and his little ones are writhing with hunger in the dark, sobbing and grinding their teeth. Surely none of these will be accused of having lit the match. In any case, the man with firm principles would do well to have some change on him in future. Nobody knows. God wears many disguises, and Fire takes on many forms. It's a Vagabond that does what it wants, without anyone knowing where it came from or where it's going. And sometimes, as was seen in the case of Sodom, it falls from the sky—perpendicularly.

LIX

I COULD BE YOUR FATHER

Je pourrais être votre père.

Of all Commonplaces this has to be the most bizarre.

In order to glimpse the enormity of it, you have to try to picture a corrupt and grimy old Jew saying to Jesus: "I could be your father."

Before Abraham was made, I am,[1] replies He who was responsible for all creation.

This phrase from the Gospel, in the mouth of a thirty year-old Man who went around raising the dead while waiting to be raised himself, doesn't make much of an impression on the cycling souls of the twentieth century. But people back then, who had to stand in order to see the Master and came and went on their own two feet, must have found it pretty extraordinary.

For at that time the idea of *paternity* being transferred from Man to God and from Time to Eternity suddenly appeared almost incomprehensible. Whether or not Abraham kept his name, you didn't know who the father was anymore, either of the one who was begotten or the one who did the begetting. And this uncertainty alone so repositioned humanity that Christianity became possible. *Pater noster.*

Today, now that we've been Christians—and what lousy Christians!—for so many generations, it's astounding to hear someone who's supposed to be reasonable, who's been baptized in the Name of the Three Divine Persons, say, even to a child, even if he himself is weighted down with centuries, "I could be your father," with the point being quite simply to express a difference in age—as though you could ever know to whom you're really speaking to or who you are yourself, and as though this stunning *conditional declaration* could have any meaning whatsoever, other than this:

"I am the Good Lord Himself, I who am speaking to you now, and you haven't the slightest suspicion!"

---

1. John 8:58.

LX

YOU ONLY DIE ONCE

On ne meurt qu'une fois.

You might as well say you only live once, which is already one time too many when you're an imbecile or an evildoer, though of course this is never the case—need we say it yet again?—when it comes to the Bourgeois.

Nevertheless, it would be interesting to know what it means to him *to die*, once or several times. I've asked before what it means to him *to live*, and the answer was so unsatisfying I've lost heart. The Bourgeois is a clever fellow who only ever says what he wants. No use complaining that the bridegroom is too handsome.

Just one thing—oh, just a trifle, really—seems clear to me, which is that he wants to avoid absolutely and at all costs heeding the Book of Revelation, which speaks of a "second death." But everyone knows what to think of the Revelation. We've had our fill and more of tales promising lakes of fire, sulfur and locusts and scorpions raining down, bottomless abysms, and the Beast with ten horns.

Voltaire, whom we don't read enough of these days, produced a victorious answer to this and many other things besides in his immortal *Philosophical Dictionary*. There, in unbelievably noble language, he explains away genius and in general any manifestation of the human soul—anything hitherto believed to be the effect of divine inspiration—as the result of extreme difficulty in moving one's bowels. An efficacious purgative is all that's required, and immediately Napoleon becomes an imbecile. Well, here's my reply to that: go take a dive into Voltaire's muck—constipation was never a problem for *him*—and see whether you don't meet death twice over.

Post-scriptum. It's worth remembering that Voltaire was no scatologist.[1]

---

1. *i.e.* as Bloy's critics often accused him of being.

LXI

BLESSED IS HE WHOSE SUFFERING HAS PASSED

Il est bienheureux, il ne souffre plus.

The Sacred Congregation of Rites, one of the blackest ulcers in the Papacy's belly, customarily demands exorbitant sums. A process of beatification costs upward of two hundred thousand francs.

The Bourgeois is beatified free of charge. As soon as he starts to stink, his parents and friends simply declare him to be blessed. It's true he doesn't get a special place on the altar, but he was never fond of altars anyway. The essential thing, for him, is to be blessed—that is to say, to suffer no more as a piece of meat. As far as the soul is concerned, he never noticed he had one.

And that's all there is to it, the process is finished. No investigation of the dead man's virtues, or whether he performed any miracles. No need for offerings, or expensive gifts, or papal bulls. The first neighbor to show up makes a very economical substitute for any promoters, judges, or cardinals, not to mention the Sovereign Pontiff. Once he's pronounced the magic words, it's clear that all is well and that the deceased has nothing more to fear.

The "progress of science," moreover, has come to help the dead along, delivering them from the agony of a premature burial. The crematorium, more reassuring than the *Requiem*, is also far more expeditious. Once upon a time, people were afraid to wake up in the hands of the awesome Judge. Today we tremble at the thought of waking up in our grave, between the four planks of a coffin. In the grip of the former fear, we would pray and pray, endlessly; our modern fright, on the other hand, is settled *tout de suite*.

Workers stuff your ashes—mixed together, I believe, with grit and cinders—in an inconsolably labeled urn, along the sides of which it sometimes refers to *when we shall meet again*. So, you "don't need anything anymore," you're among the "blessed," whose suffering has passed.

LXII

AT LEAST HE DIDN'T SUFFER

Il ne s'est pas senti mourir.

Well, well! It's not enough for the Bourgeois to suffer no more *after* death, he's determined not to suffer *during* the ordeal either. If he had any sense of style (but such things are forbidden him), he'd readily follow the example of that 18th Century *grande dame* who got drunk in order to die. I don't know exactly what degree of inebriation sufficed to comfort her or how those spirits mixed with the panicked cries of the Underworld, but one is always free to come up with his own preferred send-off.

All in all, isn't everything the Bourgeois does or wants geared toward contradicting the Word of God or of his Church? "From a sudden and unforeseen death, deliver us, O Lord," says the latter, in one of its great Litanies. It follows then that the opposite is desirable and must always be hoped for, if not demanded. For such is the great Arcana of the Bourgeois, the secret of his strength, the type of organic reaction that determines his fragrance.

He is therefore absolutely intent not to suffer as he dies. Why make a painful exit from a life built entirely around the purpose of enjoying every single breath—last one included—and which should rather be, as that pot-bellied philosopher Renan put it, a "charming walk in the park"? Why, indeed? Renan himself met just such a lovely end, dropping dead one fine day and losing his soul in the process.

LXIII

YOU'D ALMOST SAY HE WAS SLEEPING

On dirait qu'il dort.

No poor corpse lying in state, whether hero or bourgeois, has ever managed to escape this Commonplace. It's not enough to die, nay, this road, too, you still must travel. However many times I hear it, it always sends me into convulsions.

But Lord, what a sleep it is! I've seen fat and soiled and dark cadavers, seeming already to be in a state of liquefaction, terrible and appalling as Nonsense itself, but dead.

I've seen others, probably "blessed" ones, whose animal character, more or less hidden throughout their lives by the pointless twitchings of their souls, had been restored by the labor of mortal agony. There were some who resembled horses, others wolves, pigs, crocodiles, monkeys, or who knows what nightmarish beasts. One of them, I hardly dare write it down, was monstrously reminiscent of a bedbug.

I saw the body of a great poet who died weeping and on whose cheeks were left a double trace of tears.

I've seen a tiny child, who like a commander of angels must have been given permission to die, and who—mouth closed, hands in fists—looked to be waiting steadfastly for someone to summon her home.

I've also, finally, preserved the terrifying memory of a dead German soldier in the corner of a battlefield in 1870. He hadn't fallen, because someone had nailed him to a barn door with a fearsome thrust of his bayonet. The weapon, plunged quite deeply into the wood after traversing the man's chest, could no longer be withdrawn, and the murderer had contented himself with uncoupling the barrel of his rifle from the blade, leaving his victim to agonize there like a screech owl. I'll never forget the expression of horror, of terror and desperation on this man's face.

One day, a young bourgeois showed me his father-in-law, who had been laid out for several hours, surrounded by all the funerary paraphernalia. The memorial announcements had all been sent, all customary measures had been taken, the burial would take place the following day.

The departed was a retired officer from back in the good old days, a naive and honorable fellow whom I loved almost as much for his foolishness as his uprightness.

"He looks like he's sleeping," the son-in-law said. "Doesn't he?"

My first impulse was to slap the imbecile across his face, but having observed him attentively, I understood myself to be in the presence of a kind of demon. His joy at having inherited a few pennies shone forth despite his efforts. "When you're put under," he was thinking, almost certainly, "it's for a long, long time."

Having recited a silent *De profundis* to myself, I was about to flee, to escape this living person, when suddenly the dead one brought a hand to his forehead and opened his eyes…

With a cool-headedness that still astonishes me to recall, I rushed off, snuffed the candles and made everything disappear in the blink of an eye. Then I turned to the son-in-law: he'd just let out a shriek, and his frozen, vile face seemed fashioned for a citizen of hell. "Go find your wife," I told him. "You can see yourself he isn't sleeping anymore."

LXIV

SHE DIED LIKE A SAINT

Elle est morte comme une sainte.

"On the morning of October 25th, the Pilgrim found her completely terrified and distraught.

'Last night I had a frightful vision,' she said, 'which even now I am unable to dispel. I went yesterday evening to pray among the dying, and there, to my horror, I was ushered before a rather wealthy woman who I could see was about to be damned. I struggled with Satan at her bedside, but without success: he forced me back—it was too late. I cannot describe the desperation I felt when he stole this soul away, leaving her body there, folded in two, as repulsive to me as a rotting carcass. I couldn't go near it, I saw it only from above and at a certain distance, where some angels, too, were looking on.

'This woman had a husband and children. She was considered a very good person and lived in accordance with the ways of the world. She had been carrying on an illicit liaison with a priest, an old sin that had become a habit and which she had never confessed. She had received all the Sacraments: it was said she had a beautiful countenance and that she was well prepared to meet her maker. She was nevertheless in a state of agony because of the sin she had kept secret.

'Then the devil sent her one of her friends, a wretched old woman, to whom she expressed her anxieties. The friend, however, urged her to banish those thoughts and not cause a scandal. She had to let bygones be bygones, the old woman told her, she mustn't torment herself anymore now that she had received the Sacraments and shown herself a model for everyone. She mustn't arouse suspicion by sending for the priest again but rather go in peace to be with God. And with that the old friend left her alone, giving orders that the dying woman not be disturbed.

'But oh, the unfortunate creature! So near to death, her imagination was still full of desires that led her back to the priest, her accomplice in sin. And when I approached her, I found Satan in the form of this very priest, praying by her side. She herself was in the throes of agony, full of horrible thoughts, and so could not pray. The Accursed One read the Psalms to her. He cited her these verses, among others: *Let Israel hope in the Lord, because with the Lord there is mercy, and with him pletntiful redemption, etc., etc.*[1] He was furious with me. I told him to make the sign of the cross over the dying woman's mouth, but this he could not do. All my efforts were to no avail: it was too late, no one could reach her anymore. She died.

'What a horrible thing it was when Satan carried her soul away! I wept and shouted. That wretched old woman came back, consoled the dead woman's relatives who were there, and spoke of her friend's beautiful death. As I went on my way, passing over a bridge in the city, I met a few more people who were on their way to her. "Oh!" I said to myself. "If only you'd seen what I have seen, you would flee as far from her as possible!" I'm still completely sick from it, all my limbs are trembling.'"

I borrow this page from the third volume of the incomparable *Life of Anne-Catherine Emmerich,* the visionary of Dulmen, who received the mark of the stigmata, as recorded by Father Schmœger, of the Congregation of the Most Holy Redeemer.

---

1. Psalm 129:6-8.

LXV

SPEAK NO ILL OF THE DEAD

On doit le respect aux morts.

No point speaking well of the living, unless we're speaking about the powerful, in which case experience counsels us to lick their boots, however shit-encrusted they may be. But speak no ill of the dead.

The only exception being artists and poets, for whom death is no excuse. The most atrocious criminals have a right to be spoken of respectfully, and even with a certain veneration, as soon as they've passed from among the living. Why? Might it be because they have become "blessed"? That answer's too easy. Let's dig a bit further down into the depths.

I began this Exegesis by observing that the Bourgeois constantly and altogether unwittingly spouts forth expressions liable, in their absolute excessiveness, to throw the world off balance. God knows this isn't his intention, but that's the way it is, and I've undertaken the present task in the hope of demonstrating as much.

Once again, then: why does the Bourgeois affirm so obstinately that we mustn't speak ill of the dead? Perhaps because, as noted above, he has a hard time distinguishing death from life; this makes him subject to a dark apprehension urging him to claim posthumous respect for himself and for his fellows, who, with all their trappings of liveliness, are the true dead, and even the deadest of the dead!

LXVI

THE DEAD CAN'T DEFEND THEMSELVES

Les morts ne peuvent pas se défendre.

What idiocy! What hypocrisy! How can it be! They defend themselves precisely by means of the respect which is owed them and which forbids anyone speaking ill of them! Can you imagine a better defense? And it's all the more unbreachable since a continual uncertainty hangs over them. So often—I never get tired of repeating it—so often they seem still to be alive, and we have such an odd way of burying them!... Just try pissing, for example, on the statue of Gambetta, and right there on the spot you'll see them—thickening, coagulating, condensing, and finally appearing, in the form of the most fanatical repression—all the dirty shadows bent on preserving the prestige of that abominable carrion. That's what I call defending yourself.

The dead defend themselves so well, there's no way to go on living anymore. Under the pretext of collecting the respect which they claim as their right, they fill the cities and the villages besides with their effigies. Any day now, probably, they'll be invading the very homes of the townspeople, and soon enough I, who am speaking to you now, will find myself forced, under pain of severe penalty, to hang on my own walls the pernicious faces of Édouard Drumont, or doctor Maurice Peignecul,[1] or Emile Zola, a. k. a. the *Cretin of the Pyrenees.*

---

1. "Doctor Ass-comb," almost certainly referring to Maurice de Fleury, Bloy's one-time friend with whom he underwent a bitter break. Édouard Drumont was a notorious anti-Semite, whose pamphlet *La France juive* prompted Bloy to write his *Le Salut par les juifs* ("Salvation through the Jews").

LXVII

I'M NOT YOUR MAID, OR NO GOOD DEED

Je ne suis pas un domestique ou Quand on nourrit.

I've been eager to get to this one. All the fibers, all the little strands of thoughts and feelings that make up the soul of the poor Bourgeois who *doesn't* have money, lead to this one Commonplace. By this sign shall ye recognize the monster. For indeed the Bourgeois exists in penniless form as well, crawling forth from the swamp to devour his rich cousin as soon as the seven years of abundance draw to a close.

He's ugly in the way Barrès[1] is ugly: add a little grime and you couldn't tell them apart. Good Belgian education, acutely loutish behavior, and intellectual pretensions to boot. Why, he even fancies himself a kind of omniscient. The first thing you learn upon meeting him is that he knows enough Greek to translate the Napoleonic Code or the logarithmic tables into asclepiadic or choliambic verse, as necessary. He's no less familiar with Hebrew, and Syriac Aramaic holds no secrets from him. As for Sanskrit, it's more or less his native tongue. What's more, he makes no use whatsoever of all this precious knowledge. Astonishing, no? But he doesn't want to dazzle anyone with his talents, it's enough that we know he possesses them.

His nails, extraordinarily long and clipped like albatross talons, make a strange contrast with his ever-dangling lip, his pallid aspect and hard-boiled eyes. A friend advised me to beware individuals with rotten mouths and dirty feet, which this fellow also has, yet I made the mistake of ignoring his prophetic warning. Shouldn't the name alone—Edgar!—have put me on my guard?

Well, what do you expect? I thought I owed him something, and in my imprudence I went so far as to offer him the hospitality of my own home, knowing him to be in dire straits. When he insisted on making it known to me that he was nobody's servant—and in this he wasted no time—I understood the enormity of my error. But it was too late.

Besides—what else can I say?—his religious playacting got the better of me... This unmarried man, tireless imitator and transcriber of an overly

---

1. Maurice Barrès (1862–1923), novelist, politician, and another well-known anti-Semite.

celebrated writer, was himself full of texts and outpourings. In short, having never *seen* him before, I had no sense of the demoralizing effects of his outward appearance. If anything excuses my poor judgment, it is this.

Alas! He had a companion who answered to the name of Raphaële, and even a little child—a wretch foredoomed, I'm afraid, to a homicidal education. The mother was a blond wench from Flanders with soft white flesh beneath her grimy skin, flickering dust-colored eyes, and the watertight mouth of a miser inspired by La Gioconda's pursed lips. She was, I think, even more odious than her husband.

He, at least, wasn't *feeding* anyone. He was happy enough being fed (not nursed, mercifully) and having a pen nib on hand—for he goes on endlessly about this pen nib, a poor little she-devil of an old pen nib salvaged from the filth in my pencil case and which he now intends to use against me.

But the woman! O, heavenly justice! She was one of these females upon whom mankind confers a higher rank of admiration for the mere fact of suckling a babe. A languishing, lazing soul, from morning till night she would drag herself about suavely, shirt full open, with hardly the strength to call out, in a voice strained with wonder at her own unsurpassable dignity, for the attentions and gestures of respect that were her due.

It was the height of injuriousness to propose she might do something with herself.

"Have you forgotten I'm nursing?" she would shriek, this immobile chambermaid harnessed to her learned spouse. "What do you take me for, a maid?" The very idea of it seemed monstrous, a possibility no less insane than cooking split peas before the Blessed Sacrament.

I won't try to reproduce Edgar's ecstasies here. He just couldn't get over the fact that he had a wife who was nursing, and, his lip hanging there, he gazed at this spectacle all day long, filled with lyrical indignation that the abundance of rare meats and succulent morsels he'd hoped to find at my table (for her sake but above all for his) was not, in fact, forthcoming. For let me tell you, this Hellenist packed it away like a Homeric warrior.

For three months I sheltered and stuffed the gracious couple. A week hadn't gone by, and I'd already had enough. But it was winter. My wife, who had yet to earn the horrible calumnies she'd have heaped upon her later, begged me to be patient, and we took pity on the child. In the end, God remembered us, and a two-fold miracle was accomplished. Believing they'd found better accommodations, the vermin set us free, and some alms fell from the sky to cover the enormous expense.

Just last month, Edgar, whom I believed to be in the lowest depths, reappeared to squeeze me—*in the Name of Blessed Mary!*—for a handsome sum. Everyone knows I'm a beggar, and everyone takes advantage of the fact. My expression of surprise and my admission that I couldn't help him immediately earned me a boorish letter, which I've held on to like a precious artifact, a contribution to the history of the unmoneyed Bourgeois at the beginning of the twentieth century.

Turn up your nose at the bread you've gorged yourself on from the table of poor folk, then send them, as compensation, a flood tide of obscenities wherein every other minute you piously invoke the name of God; get matched up with an idiot who manages the sublime act of breastfeeding and who, as an added bonus, presses the bounds of heroism all the way to *not* being anybody's maid, divinely equipped though she is to empty chamber pots and rinse them with care: such are the broad outlines of this journeyman of your own species, who threatens you, O rich Bourgeois, who comes from the Low Lands to swallow you up.[2]

---

2. Bloy's own footnote in the original: "See *The Son of Louis XVI*, chapter X, in which I examine the serious question of *Domestic Service* in all its depth."

LXVIII

I DON'T NEED ANYBODY

Je n'ai besoin de personne.

Therefore, I am God. This is the remarkable and *necessary* conclusion of more or less everything the bourgeois says. I've pointed it out more than once. The Commonplaces are thus interpenetrating, like the collapsing tubes of a telescope, or like a commercial freighter ramming into the cars of a high-speed train. It's fun for the spectator, but tedious over time.

Redundancy is the all but inevitable pitfall of a book like this. And yet I hope the strength will be given me to see it through to the end. Since I don't have the honor of being bourgeois myself, it costs me nothing to confess that I need *everybody,* beginning precisely with the Bourgeois, who provides me my material and, belonging as he does to this changeable species of ours, rewards the attentive observer with a certain measure of variety.

LXIX

GREAT SORROWS ARE SILENT

Les grandes douleurs sont muettes.

Which means that the silence of Monsieur Ignibus, the famous hatter who just buried his wife in a cemetery outside Paris (having poisoned her with sombrero scrapings), expresses an even greater sorrow than the *Lamentations* of Jeremiah, which contains no less than a hundred and fifty Verses, high as those biblical mounts upon each of whose summits a lion roars.

Of this, there isn't the slightest doubt. One might reply that the Bourgeois, an expert in sorrow (none knows better than he how to inflict it on others), doesn't much care for frightful tears, and the rantings of Hecubas are disagreeable to him. He's a simple man.

He's just as likely as the next fellow to be an imbecile or a scoundrel—that's human fragility for you—but the sorrows that prey on *him* can only be great and silent. No two ways about it. Try to picture a rubber-tube manufacturer, a maker of box springs for bed bases, someone who puts the gum on letter paper, a first class road surveyor, or even a supervising architect; and now try to picture him emitting a blood-curdling wail or letting fly some Sophoclean lyricism to lament the demise of one of his family members!

LXX

QUO VADIS?

"Quo vadis?"

Allow us here to quickly insert a literary Commonplace that will be gone by tomorrow but which has held such raging sway for so many months. Oh, I have no intention of talking about that silly book,[1] so roundly condemned by its very success and which Catholics and Protestants alike admire unanimously—which is, intellectually speaking, the shame to end all shames. We've even seen priests cite passages from the pulpit!...

I only wanted to share an anecdote with you. Here goes. The other day, in Lagny Station, two ecclesiastics belonging, I would like to believe, to the intelligent Diocese of Meaux, were hurrying along in front of me. One of them, in more of a rush than the other, suddenly dashed toward a urinal. *Quo vadis?* his colleague shouted after him. I didn't hear the answer, which was in any event a matter of indifference to me.

---

1. *Quo Vadis: A Narrative of the Time of Nero* (1896), by the Nobel prize-winning Polish writer Henryk Sienkiewicz, first published in French translation in 1900.

LXXI

THE PRETTIEST GIRL IN THE WORLD
CAN ONLY GIVE WHAT SHE HAS

La plus jolie fille du monde ne peut donner que ce qu'elle a.

We were in the vicinity of Sully-sur-Loire, pinned down by the Germans. The French army, victorious only a few days before, was crumbling apart along every road. A massive debacle. The cold was terrible, demoralizing.

One unhappy night, four young men belonging to I don't know which line regiment came like wolves upon an isolated house close by the woods. They didn't know where their column was anymore and in fact had no interest in knowing, having fallen, as a result of fatigue, cold, and hunger, into a state of complete despondency. To eat something, anything, and to sleep someplace warm, these were their sole ambitions now, their final goal.

Unfortunately, the house they had just entered, the door of which they had only to give a little push, did not appear to be the place they were dreaming of. It seemed to them even colder within than without, and a meticulous inspection turned up not a crust of bread, nor a slice of lard, nor a single potato, nor a bottle of wine, nor anything else that might be chewed or swallowed. Obviously the shelter had been abandoned weeks ago.

It's true, this search was conducted with a few miserable matches and the butt of a candle. No hope of making a fire, wood and coal were no less scarce than provisions for the gullet, and they had no tools for carving up the woodwork. It crossed their minds to set fire to the house itself, but they thought better of this almost right away—nothing does such a poor job keeping people warm as an outright blaze, and, after all, the protection of this shack, such as it was, was worth more than a spectacle of constellations. Besides, the sensible thing was not to make themselves too conspicuous. There was no telling who else might be in the vicinity. Dying of weariness and more famished than ever, they hunkered down at last on some old mattresses as solid as haystacks and did their best to fall asleep.

Their uneasy rest didn't last long. The door, which they hadn't taken the precaution to lock behind them, opened violently again, clearing the way for three big sharpshooting devils, pursued a short distance behind by a Bavarian patrol whose commander, an officer of abominable aspect, kept trained upon them the yellow beam of his lantern. A volley of rifle fire accompanied their disappearance into the fortress. The sleeping men were on their feet in the blink of an eye, the door shut again, locked, and barricaded instantaneously.

Daybreak was long in coming, but until then these seven men were left in peace. They had time enough to get to know each other, and not one was any less famished than the next. The shuddering dawn glimmered faintly that the siege was underway.

The poor boys tried to defend themselves, but what could they do against so many? Their sanctuary was soon overrun. One of the snipers had protection enough from the holy angels to be disemboweled in the course of the battle. The others, cornered into too narrow a space and exhausted, moreover, by their misfortunes, allowed themselves to be taken. Their scores were settled soon enough. The Prussians showed little consideration for the snipers, or for the fighters cut off from their company, and in those days gunfire was the answer to everything.

So here's what happened. At the last moment, the youngest of these wretches asked for no greater mercy than *a piece of bread to eat* before dying. The Prussian leader, an atrociously ugly character, as I mentioned above, wanted to prove that he had at least some spirit in him—and even some French spirit—and so he made a gesture with his hand toward the rifles of the firing squad and said these words: "Ze brettiest girl in ze vorld can only gif vot she hass…"

Followed immediately by the signal to fire away.

Whenever a bourgeois says something to me about the prettiest girl in the world, I think how we have no idea what death is, and that thirty years later this poor child might still be hungry.

LXXII

YOU CAN'T EXPECT THE IMPOSSIBLE

À l'impossible nul n'est tenu.

Napoleon, the greatest spouter of Commonplaces the world has ever seen, declared that the word *impossible* doesn't exist in French. The present generation is much less dramatic and has a more comprehensive dictionary. Unlike what was happening in 1805 or 1809, today many things have become impossible. But could any one of these things be as impossible as giving money to whomever, for whatever reason? Even irrepressibly lustful people will recoil at the idea of handing over what they've been paid for selling out their Savior.

I hope you'll be grateful for the absolutely unknown anecdote that follows:

Twenty or twenty-five years ago, the Sacred Congregation of Rites, on which the Roman Church so prides itself and which abhors any form of simony, as shall be seen, demanded the insignificant gratuity of 175,000 francs in exchange for playing a useful role in the Cause of the Beatification of Christopher Columbus.[1]

All other obstacles had been swept aside. Six hundred bishops had signed the *postulatum*, and the ecclesiastical world knew that this immensely just act, so ardently—and recently—desired by Pius IX, who was its true promoter two generations ago, had been approved by the Vatican Council almost without opposition.

The postulator,[2] since deceased, could have paid. He was an extremely old man, at death's door from one day to the next but soaked in the bourgeois Styx and invulnerable to any spirit of renunciation.

"Why won't you pay?" I said to him in '92, in the times of those famous celebrations of the quadricentennial of the Discovery of America. "You've been working for this cause, your sole objective, for forty years now. You're old, you have no children, you're going to die. You'll have enough to subsist

---

1. See Bloy's *Le révélateur du globe: Christophe Colomb et sa béatification future*. Paris: A. Sauton, 1884.

2. The person in question here is Bloy's friend Le Comte Antoine-François-Félix Roselly de Lorgues, who took a passionate interest in Christopher Columbus, but not to the same degree as Léon Bloy. He preferred to live peacefully rather than go to too much trouble for "the cause"—hence Bloy's reproachfulness. —J. P.

honorably till the end of your days, even after having indulged these loathsome judges. Don't deprive your life's last hour of this consolation."

"My dear friend," he replied in a faraway voice, like a captive insect, *"you can't expect the impossible.* It's precisely because I'm so old that I can't do it. When I was young, who can say, but now... just think of it!"

Not long after this refusal, which Someone was probably waiting for, a rapid succession of disastrous speculations whittled his fortune down by the sum total of *one hundred seventy-five thousand francs.*

LXXIII

FOREWARNED IS FOREARMED

Un homme averti en vaut deux.

I forewarn you therefore, dear Sir, that you shall, within such and such a time, receive twelve dozen slaps in the face and an equal number of bootkicks to the backside, not to mention a few little supplementary treatments to fancy up the ball. All told, it won't be too much for the resignation and strength of soul of *two*[1] men to bear. So that's all in order now, you can't say you haven't been warned.

Now I think of it, this might be a way to get troop numbers up during wartime, or at least to *double* the steadfastness, even the agility, of our soldiers, in case of misfortune. It's a question worth studying.

---

1. Plays on the French original, *Un homme averti en vaut deux*. Literally: "A man forewarned is worth two."

LXXIV

WHAT DO YOU EXPECT? WE'RE ONLY HUMAN!

Que voulez-vous! l'homme est l'homme.

What a good little boy Pilate is, and how worthy of love when we compare him to the considerable multitude of hand-washers out there! The other day this phrase, dragged out over and over again for two dozen centuries, was served up to me by a kindly bourgeois who appeared to have clean hands, in order to justify the behavior of a savage bourgeois, about whom I was so childish as to share my extreme indignation with the first fellow. He didn't dare to add, as in the telling of Saint John, *Ecce rex vester*, Behold your king!, because the Bourgeois never puts what is within himself outside of himself, but how could he not have been thinking it, deep down, in his private-most place?

The man he showed me, vaguely, was dressed in the bloody purple of the weak, with bloody tears streaming from his frightful crown. Yet there is only one man who is truly Man, and it's terrible to evoke him in this way, for one isn't always able to distinguish very well between He who takes things upon himself and he who is the thing taken, between He who saves and he who kills. What an horrific situation for a destroyer of souls, to have stooped so low he can no longer maintain the appearance of being a *man* except by way of an unspeakable masquerade, cloaking himself in the inexpressibly holy garments of Gabbatha!

LXXV

HEAVEN IS NOT AVERSE TO COMPROMISE

Il est avec le ciel des accommodements.

Maybe heaven isn't, but the Bourgeois is, especially when it comes to Molière. You mustn't touch! Do whatever you like, but not that.

Profane the sanctuaries, the Holy Relics, the dreaded Sacrament of the altar. So be it, but don't lift a finger against Molière.

This law is all the more remarkable for the fact that the Bourgeois is entirely ignorant of Molière's work. Basically, he knows that the famous man talked a lot about cuckolds—which flatters him—and that he was the author of a comedy entitled *Tartuffe,* in which the infamy of religious devotion is laid bare. He's unshakably convinced that Louis XIV, brought to heel by so much genius, had the man to dinner one day, and that the whole court was in a daze of admiration. I believe, in fact, that this is the sole detail of Louis XIV's reign the Bourgeois would be able to cite, and his undying gratitude for this royal meal reflects the profound sensation he has, that he had been invited himself—in the person of Molière!

In my greenest youth, nearing on thirty-five years ago, Jules Vallès held a sort of referendum against Molière. There was a register in the weekly newspaper, *La Rue,* over which the future agitator presided, where everyone was invited to join in an energetic protest against *The Misanthrope.* I recall there being a bit of a hue and cry in the serious papers, but very few signatures. The Bourgeois was no more sovereign then than he is today, which in any case would be impossible, only he was somewhat less poorly educated and seemed to read now and then. But I find our own age to be much more beautiful, since it's a time of faith. We adore Molière now as the Athenians adored their unknown God.

LXXVI

WE'LL KNOW EACH OTHER IN HEAVEN

Au ciel on se reconnaît.

While we're there, let's send this next Commonplace to the great beyond. It goes without saying, surely, but this one comes straight from the sacristy.

We'll recognize one another in heaven. That is to say, we'll no longer have to suffer the boredom of proving our identity to such a great mass of people once we've settled into that Beatific Place—where bourgeois ladies and gentlemen necessarily go. We'll be recognized there, and we'll recognize others right away. It will be part of our interminable happiness. And it will be a way for us to avoid contact with all sorts of upstarts and schemers who, not having been bourgeois back on earth, might claim to be so eternally in heaven—the insolence! But this has all been so well sorted out, there's no reason to give it another instant of our attention.

LXXVII

A PRIEST IS A MAN LIKE ANY OTHER

Les prêtres sont des hommes comme les autres.

"Like any other" is a euphemism, certainly. And it's quite certain that a man who practices self-restraint and says mass every day is markedly inferior to others. If it weren't for his great goodness, the Bourgeois would say (with more exactitude and firmness) that a priest is a man *unlike* any other. Precisely the opposite. But it's right and proper to be generous and not run anybody over, and, after all, Bourgeois thought isn't an *automobile*.

Moreover, not all priests are alike. There are still—thank God!—a rather large number who don't go about with their heads in the clouds, who favor what is serious, solid, comfortable. These ones make the others go down easier. You can have them over for a visit, invite them to dinner, have them run errands for you, give them your packages for safekeeping—make use of them, in short—which changes something in these fussbudgets, who are always going on about sacerdotal dignity.

Some even have excellent positions and earn a lot of money. Flat on our bellies before these ones, naturally. In principle, though, we don't like to go too hard on the priests. Life is short. And let's not forget that the Commonplace in question here is a counter-truth, an ironical phrase full of mystery, and may well harbor death within.

LXXVIII

EVERY MAN FOR HIMSELF AND THE DEVIL TAKE THE HINDMOST

Chacun pour soi et le bon Dieu pour tous.

Madame Plutarch, proprietress of the shop previously known as "Plutarch and Uncle, Purveyors of Stationery and Religious Articles," does her daily meditation at the local parish, in the presence of the Blessed Sacrament. She's a very pious woman.

"Beloved son of the Almighty," she says, with the help of one of those books put out by Mame or Poussielgue, whose praises have been adequately sung. "O my most gentle Master, who came into the world to wash away our sins, have pity on those who persist in their iniquity and moan in the shadow of death... I ask you also to send a few more people our way for this year's Jubilee. If there's ever going to be a chance to sell off the rest of our old cotton scapulars, that would be it. They're getting all moth-eaten, you know, and we still have quite a few left...

"Stainless Lamb, who have sacrificed Yourself so lovingly for us sinners, have mercy on our souls and deliver us from the devil's bondage through the glory of your sacrifice... I'm rather afraid I've ordered too many porcelain stoups. Some of our clients complain they're too expensive, but it's a profitable item and there's really no way for me to let them go for any less. There'd be nothing left for me to do but close up shop. Fortunately, they break easily and the churches can't do without them. We make up for it on volume...

"Our sins, O divine Savior, have armed your executioners with the instruments of your torture... The truth is, business is business, and there'd be no way to make ends meet if we just gave the merchandise away. Besides, during the off-season we barely manage to sell a catechism, or a bottle of ink, or a ream of paper. If now and then, here and there, we put out a little novel, something a bit on the trashy side, a little (more or less) see-through deck of cards, I mean, my God! it's not our fault if people buy them, is it? Besides, as you know, that's not the sort of business I conduct with just anyone, only well-dressed gentlemen of a certain age. Where's the harm in that? Ah! sweet Jesus, don't ever go into retail!

"This mystery teaches us the mortification of the flesh. It was in order to emulate the scourging of our Savior that the saints undertook such bloody disciplines... Oh! the discipline business isn't going so well either! We're killing ourselves just to sell a few lousy cords of St. Francis. As for horse-hair, demand has completely dried up, that much I understand. We had a few old hair shirts left over, which once belonged to the pastor of Ars (that's the story we told anyway, but everybody does that in our line of work), and we had such a hassle getting rid of them we swore we were done with them for good...

"I acknowledge, O Jesus, that your death destroyed the sinfulness in me. Your resurrection has delivered me from the tomb of vices where for so long I slept the slumber of the dead... Actually, our company is going to be expanding, in spite of everything. The suppository manufacturer isn't doing much business anymore. I'll be damned if he doesn't let us take over his lease at half-price. Besides, he's a Dreyfusard[1] and we've helped in every way we can to see he goes bankrupt. It'll be a real godsend. As for his daughter, who's dying of tuberculosis, it's for the best you're putting her out of her misery. We've tried to do well by her, but no good deed goes unpunished. Can you believe the father accused of us of killing her, letting her stand in the shop all day long—as though it were our fault if our neighbors got sick! Every man for himself and the Devil take the hindmost. When she wasn't able to work anymore, we showed her the door, which was the only proper thing to do. You would have done the same yourself, my Redeemer, isn't it so? Everyone's spreading these awful rumors about me now, but with the comfort of your grace I'll bear my cross to the bitter end. My dear Lord's love shall suffice me in this vale of tears, and in the blessed eternity to come. Amen."

---

1. Bloy had a complicated relationship to Judaism but strongly rejected anti-Semitism. His line on the Dreyfus Affair was, "I am neither for Dreyfus, nor against Dreyfus; I'm against pigs."

LXXIX

GO ALONG YOUR MERRY WAY

Aller son petit bonhomme de chemin.

"Following a relentless siege of seven months, Alexander the Great succeeded in capturing the impregnable city of Tyr. As punishment for the Tyrian resistance, he crucified two thousand of its inhabitants who until then had escaped the fury of his soldiers. After which, in the direction of Egypt, he continued along his merry way."

Thus spake, some forty years ago, a dignified history professor of the Périgueux Lycée, who hardly registered the horrifying jokes he inflicted on his students almost every day.

This "merry way" has remained in my memory, glued to the name of Alexander and to this scholar's face as with a kind of resin. There is no way anymore to separate them, and, owing to the phenomenon of mental association and the lineage of ideas, I cannot hear this Commonplace without immediately seeing the most heroic characters parading away, light of foot, having accomplished some grandiose atrocity. Napoleon, for example, after the Battle of Berezina, or, if you prefer, the lovable Nero who, much as I'd like it to be otherwise, was not merely an imbecile, but an imbecilic master of the universe who went no less than the others along his merry way, which, as Tacitus recounted, was planted up and down with burning Christians, *ut cum defecisset dies, in usum nocturni luminis urerentur.*[1]

The Bourgeois, himself now heir and successor of these terrifying figures, goes along his merry way toward death—with dung to light his path.

---

1. From the *Annals* of Tacitus XV, XLIV: "...[who] served when day declined as nocturnal lights." —J. P.

LXXX

NOT WORTH A DEVIL

Ne pas valoir le Diable.

Where is the gentleman, then, who can boast of being worth so much? Devil he may be, he's still an angel, and the leader of a great many angels. If this or that civil engineer or police sergeant understands this phrase to mean that so and so isn't worth much, or anything at all, then he's mistaken to an astonishing degree. To claim that such and such individual isn't as rich as a billionaire doesn't imply that he's a pauper. You might well not be worth a Devil and yet nonetheless—without breaking a sweat—amass the moral and intellectual value of an infinite number of bourgeois. I wonder, what should we think of someone who *is* worth a Devil—or even *the* Devil…?

We really should pay more attention to the things we say. The Devil doesn't like when we compare ourselves to him, even if it's to declare we aren't worth as much as he—and words can summon him, you know. A little known writer[1] once said, "When we're not speaking to God or for God, it's the Devil we're speaking to. And he listens to us in fearsome silence…"

---

1. Bloy himself, in *Le révélateur du globe*, p. 18.

LXXXI

IT'S TOO GOOD TO BE TRUE
(THE BRIDE IS MUCH TOO BEAUTIFUL)

Se plaindre que la mariée est trop belle.

Try getting your average bourgeois to understand that this could indeed be good reason for complaint, and that a bride's excessive beauty might entail certain inconveniences! How far they are from fearing such a thing, much less moaning about it! They require wives of perfect beauty. All I have to do is look around me: it's unbelievable, really. Alarming. Dazzling! Where these pigs go to find such women, I have no idea.

Well then, being so firmly established among the beautiful, beauty is, naturally, the only thing they see, the only thing they think about anymore. This or that bit of business becomes for them a bride who must be beautiful, who can never be *too* beautiful, and whose beauty appears to them a monstrous thing for anyone to complain about, especially when these whiners are about to be taken for everything they're worth.

Some day there will be a Bride who will rattle the gates of heaven as she draws near, whose great beauty will be indistinguishable from a bolt of lightning. She is the One of whom it is written: "she shall laugh in the latter day."[1] She will arrive in the form of God's Judgment, and no one will have time to complain that she is much too beautiful. But can we imagine the bourgeois capable of sensing her approach?

---

1. Proverbs 31:25.

LXXXII

KILLING TIME

Tuer le temps.

In bourgeois parlance killing time simply means—need I even say it?—having fun. When the Bourgeois gets bored, time *lives*, or comes back to life. Either you'll understand this or you won't, but that's the way it is. When the Bourgeois has fun, we're entering the realm of the eternal. For Bourgeois entertainments are like death.

LXXXIII

ALWAYS READY WITH A JOKE

Avoir le mot pour rire.

When we think of people who tend to be ready with a joke, morticians, prison guards, bailiffs, surgeons, butchers, come readily to mind. It appears their honoroble professions demand it.

Villiers de l'Isle-Adam,[1] who was a passionate spectator of capital punishments and who was considered an enlightened amateur by the guillotinistes, claimed to have overheard the headsman tell one of his clients, tapping the man joyfully on the shoulder ten minutes before the blade was to fall, "I'm spoiling you, my friend, I'm spoiling you!"

He had just treated him to one of those little gallantries executioners guard the secret of. The rattle of that headcutter's voice lodged in Villiers' ear, and the sound, he alleged, was *irresistible*—make of that qualifying adjective what you will.

---

1. Auguste Villiers de l'Isle-Adam (1838–1889), author of the influential *Contes cruels* and *L'Ève future,* was Léon Bloy's friend and mentor.

LXXXIV

SECURE YOUR CHILDREN'S FUTURE

Assurer l'avenir de ses enfants.

Isn't it odd that, in all this long time fathers have been taking care of their children's future, the children haven't given any thought to the future of their fathers? Who was the first to point this out, I wonder, and what *future* could that anonymous person have had in mind? The Bourgeois is astounded whenever a question is presented in this way—yet what could be more simple? We just have to allow for the possibility of a father being engendered by his child.[1]

> In vain does blood make me descendant of them all,
> Were I to write their stories, they'd all descend from me.
> (Alfred de Vigny, "L'Esprit pur.")

Cornelian verses, almost forgotten today, whose splendor gave the poet-gentleman Alfred de Vigny some comfort in his disgrace at not having been born in a retail shop, and for not having been able thence to bequeath a ready clientele upon his wealthy, cretinous children.

The Bourgeois, a happier fellow, congratulates himself in another language. Whomever his ancestors are, he'd have no idea how to descend from them, nor indeed how to climb back up to them. His entire lineage for centuries on end maintains an absolute horizontality along the lowest possible geometric plane, and, barring some miracle, this posture is *secured* into the future for anyone he might bring into the world.

Barring some miracle—obviously. Nonetheless, it wouldn't be impossible for some exceptional being to spring forth from this alluvium of excreta. But what sort of future might this progeny bestow upon its fathers? The phenomenal drollness of *that* problem, I leave to you, dear readers—those of you at any rate who were born upon joyful hills.

---

1. See LIX above: "I could be your father."

LXXXV

DO HONOR TO ONE'S BUSINESS[1]

Faire honneur à ses affaires.

The word "business" always bothers me. I've tried, from the very beginning of this Exegesis, to say something about it, but have so far only succeeded in demonstrating my own impotence. What strikes me as particularly detestable about the blasted word is its mysteriousness. Impossible to penetrate. To "do honor to one's business" is one of the most frequently repeated and certainly one of the least heeded sayings we have.

What does *honor* have to do with it? I ask this of you, O wise ones. Now, to do honor to *somebody*, that's an intelligible locution. Example. A pirate armed to the teeth. You bend over backwards to prove what esteem and profound consideration you have for him. That one should treat every bastard who has money or power *with honor*, why, that's the guiding principle of the bourgeois conscience. But to *do honor to one's business*, it's a difficult text to parse.

I know as well as you do that it means—in language unintelligible to the pure in spirit—that we should make sure to repay our bills of exchange, our promissory notes, and every other filth of that kind. Nor am I unaware that any bane to the poor, the manager of a cathouse, say, or a loan shark charging a hundred and fifty or two hundred percent interest, is doing honor to his business when he settles those transactions with maximum exactness. Well! What can I tell you? This over-accentuated way of expressing a platitude distresses me deeply.

---

1. *Affaires* in French has a different usage than *business* (though both are similarly flexible), while *faire honneur* essentially translates as *doing justice*, which is already a kind of metaphor. To "be a credit" to one's profession, or to conduct one's business honorably, would be more idiomatic in English, but either version would spoil the rest of Bloy's word play. Hence the clunkier but hopefully more illustrative translation.

LXXXVI

MAKE A HOLE IN THE MOON[1] AND CARVE OUT A NICHE FOR YOURSELF

Faire un trou à la lune. Faire son trou.

Identical in the Absolute, identical in the Infinite. No one will ever say: Make a hole in the sun, or in the Earth, or in Mars, or even in Venus. One only makes holes in the moon, and only on the moon, which, truth be told, is itself nothing more than a vast system of holes and deep caverns, does one make a hole (call it a niche) for oneself.

That, at least, is the testimony of a contemporary English novelist who, not long ago, was fortunate enough to take advantage of an altogether unique opportunity to *visit* the moon. He even brought back from his journey some enormous bars of virgin gold for all of London to admire. Now at last we know that gold is to be found flowering over the moon's surface and is no less common upon that satellite than stone.[2]

Thus it turns out, following generations of cashiers, that the bourgeois metaphor of a happy passage through the moon when absconding with someone else's property is corroborated by the experimental evidence. Thus is it demonstrated, with a precision I dare qualify as astronomical, that the idea of the *hole* is inherent to the general idea of human prosperity. The Bourgeois has guessed correctly—he always does—but this time he hurls us into the heavens.

---

1. Meaning to *skip town*, (i.e. without paying one's creditors). The legibility of Bloy's exegesis, which focuses on both *hole* and *moon*, depends on a literal translation.
2. See H. G. Wells's *The First Men on the Moon*, translated into French by Henry D. Davray and published by Mercure de France.

LXXXVII

BURN THE CANDLE AT BOTH ENDS

Brûler la chandelle par les deux bouts.

Monsieur Need understood the peroration all the better since it was punctuated by a dazzling punch. That other Expression, about *seeing thirty-six candles*[1] had never been more completely justified, for the puncher had muscle to match his dialectics.

Monsieur Need is one of these *thinkers* that domestic animals are alarmed to see *roaming free*. The most original thing about him is that, like everybody else, he forsook God during the illuminating epoch of his adolescence. Very few things remained hidden from him after that. Having spent his life far from the sacerdotal world, he knows all about priests—that goes without saying—and he knows exactly what a person ought to think about their priestly little schemes. Monsieur Need sucks greedily upon the already well-sucked eighteenth century and passes, in the capital of his minor prefecture, for a first-rate intelligence. He's always ready to hold forth on the Inquisition, the Saint-Bartholomew's Day massacre, the Revocation of the Edict of Nantes, etc., in phrases that were already looking moldy around 1820, and he expresses himself vociferously against the fanaticism of two or three devoted old hags who attend the local parish church *religiously*.

The only thing left to do is turn this orator into a deputy. He'd know how to put an end to this religion business, if only he were in charge! It probably isn't so bad—or evil, if you like—to have sent a fair number of nuns and friars looking for other work. This Statesman's gizzard swells at the thought that perhaps, from now on, the Carmelite order of penitents or the Knights Hospitaller will be left wandering with nothing to eat. But what spineless execution! What timidity! What a lack of decisiveness! What impotence! When what really needed to be done was chuck the whole thing out in a flash…

Monsieur Need was at this very point in his speech, in a crowded *Café du Commerce,* when the sacristan, a fiery fellow who'd come to wet his whistle, asked him brusquely if he was ready to "button that lip." The orator, stifled and stricken dumb, gave no answer.

---

1. The French equivalent of "seeing stars."

"In that case I've got a little speech for you," the churchman continued. "You made yours, now I'll make mine. The first thing I have to tell you is that you're an imbecile, and that you're burning your candle at both ends. You go on braying here from dawn till dusk, often till midnight, against the priests, against the church, against the ceremonies and against the bells whose ringing exasperates you as though you were a demon, and even, finally, against the nuns and friars. At the same time, you've sent your two daughters to a boarding school in Paris with the Sisters of the Visitation. You must, I suppose, use your tongue somewhat differently there. Personally, I couldn't give a damn, let's be clear about that. Only I find the way you contradict yourself in the space of a few short minutes—in the time it takes for a trip to Paris and back—a bit odious. It's disgusting to lie like you do, continually and indiscriminately, intentionally throwing everyone into confusion. The good news is you're burning yourself, perfect idiot that you are, from both sides at once. I'll say it again and I have no problem saying it to your face. But allow me to introduce myself: Charlemagne Dasconaguerre, former sergeant of the Reichshoffen Cuirassiers and now a churchgoing Christian, what your like would call a *sanctimonious prig*..."

I couldn't see the smack that followed this harangue—I was sitting in the back of the café and without a decent view—but what a smack it was! Had Monsieur Need scoffed at the man, or ventured a threatening gesture? Whatever happened, it left him with a broken jaw.

LXXXVIII

DON'T COUNT YOUR CHICKENS…

Vendre la peau de l'ours…

Yes, I know, you mustn't count them. Not if you haven't sold them first. Good advice. Count any creature you like, so long as you've found a buyer, everyone knows that, but don't count chickens, and above all don't count the big Chicken in the sky. As commercial operations go, chicken-counting seems a rather dangerous one. What's more, it's the only one the Bourgeois advises us not to engage in. A notable exception.

Yet here's something that's not quite clear to me. If you aren't supposed to count these chickens unless you've already sold them, you must *really* not be supposed to *give* them away, there being nothing more contrary to the bourgeois spirit than the act of giving. And therefore you must keep them, your chickens. What a business! It's true, this thorny Commonplace is conditional. The authorities assure us that anyone is free to count his chickens so long as they have already hatched, which is a bad joke, really, even for the Bourgeois. He must be having one over on us.

LXXXIX

LOSE YOUR ILLUSIONS

Perdre ses illusions.

That's the first thing on the agenda. It should be the only thing, so much it encompasses all the others. A bourgeois who hasn't lost his illusions is like a hippopotamus with wings. Illusions, when it comes down to it, are whatever can't be digested. The stockbreeders are right about this much: no illusion will ever be worth a sack of potatoes when it comes to fattening up the pigs. No doubt, no doubt. But there again, we run into a problem.

How should we understand this word, *illusion?* Are there certain illusions peculiar to the bourgeois and others that only affect heroes and poets? Yes or no, should we say that a great artist is in thrall to illusions so extravagant that he *needs* to lose them if, for example, he believes, with the unsurpassable Hanotaux, that one has to "*choose* a career," or that beet juice, ounce for ounce, is no less precious than Michelangelo's *Moses?*

I posed this question to a clerk in a pawnbroker's shop, and he asked if I was pulling his chain. He was right. There's a risk no matter what you answer.

XC

SUFFER LIKE A MARTYR

Souffrir le martyre.

He's in agony, he's suffering like a martyr. Every time a bourgeois atones on his deathbed for the depravities of his existence, he's a martyr. It never fails. And so once again we dishonor an otherwise admirable idea and expression. Once upon a time the word martyr meant *witness,* and the martyrs endured horrible torments, by choice and of their own free will, in order to bear witness to the crucified Truth. Things have changed considerably since then.

The martyrdom of the Entrepreneur, quite distinct from the Virgin variety, consists of his suffering very much against his will, howling and blaspheming all the way to his stinking death. Good riddance, as far as his proud family is concerned, and forevermore he'll be referred to as one of the "blessed," but I seem to have a hard time including him among the *Semen christianorum* of the dread African Father.[1] The serums and sanies of this bourgeois invalid are more likely to engender plague.

Yet there are words which know neither rest nor pardon, superhuman words that roam like wolves around those who abuse them. These words absolutely cannot help but express, however they will and at whatever price, an indisputable reality. Either a man is the voluntary witness of *He who is,* or inevitably he must be the involuntary and fantastical assistant of *He who is not*—who also wants his martyrs.

---

1. A reference to Tertullian (*Apologia* 50, 13): *Sanguis martyrum, semen christianorum* ("The blood of martyrs is the seed of [future] Christians"). —J. P.

XCI

HIDDEN AWAY IN THE CLOISTER

S'ensevelir dans le cloître.

This Expression belongs to a small number of tropes held over from the more or less Christian education that was still on offer forty odd years ago. Generally, a person "hides himself away in the cloister" after having "drunk the chalice to the dregs," having had "a heavy cross to bear," or having "climbed the hill of Calvary." I've known a few illustrious men who were "crucified" on a rather regular basis, but being hidden away in the cloister is the last and final blow. One especially makes up his mind to do it when he has crimes to pay for. It's what's called proverbial.

The idea that someone would rush off into the religious life as though into a chasm of joy, is as foreign to the spouse of a Bourgeois woman as gallstones to a three-thousand-year-old mummy. The horrifying crimes of the Benedictines, together with the heartrending remorse of the Capuchins, act as a most fortuitous foil to the uprightness of this or that deputy or magistrate—which, let us note in passing, renders the present, idiotic zeal for abolishing them all the more inexplicable.

But now I think of it, might there not be a kind of cloister, previously undreamt-of, analogous to the one referred to above but which would serve to shut up good-natured fellows with nothing to reproach themselves for? Doesn't the Unknown, which demands its martyrs, also demand its monks? There are signs enough pointing to the affirmative, which must make the Bourgeois tremble. None shall rid me of the conviction that it is absolutely essential to choose between the two monasteries: the one for the rabble, which has naturally devolved to the Trappists and the Carthusians, and the other for Decent People—the key to which the Devil shall, on the Last Day, toss into the Abyss.

XCII

NIT-PICK

Chercher la petite bête.

One might think we were talking about a famous painting by Murillo.[1] But with the Bourgeois, it's never a matter of a work (*œuvre*) of art—unless you're talking about a metal bridge, or a tunnel, or any other hideous *necessity* of that ilk, which preeminent representatives of the bourgeoisie (that is to say, Engineers of bridges and roads) haven't the slightest qualm referring to as works (*travaux*) of art.

At play here is something else entirely. The picking of nits is a metaphor, a poor she-devil louse of a bourgeois metaphor such as are still deployed in the Merchant Marine and among the marketplace criers, or among our traveling salesmen of recent times. The merchant looking for an accounting error that disfavors one of his buyers is a man picking nits—in short, a man who is lost. It's as though he were hunting tigers with a multiplication table and an umbrella.

---

1. The painting in question, in fact, is Bartolomé Esteban Murillo's *Le petit mendiant* or *The Young Beggar* (1645–50), also often called *The Lice-ridden Boy* because he is depicted delousing himself. —J. P.

XCIII

HOLD OUT YOUR HAND

Tendre la main.

This takes me back to the clergy in the Diocese of Meaux. I made an experiment one day of begging alms from the priest of a parish directly dependent on the deanery of Lagny. He refused me (need I even say it?) with speeches of oil and honey, sweet and cold as the moon.

Though still a young man, the ecclesiastic in question has the physiognomy of an old rat and, so it appears, the morals to boot. Round as one of those doughnut-cushions the bureaucrats use to ward off hemorrhoids[1] and glistening like a lump of fat behind a perpetually inquisitive nose capped by two black and shiny little nailhead eyes, this Virginal abbot is the very model of a bourgeois priest.

He likes to think himself an archaeologist, telling anyone who will listen that he, too, is so prolific the publishers can't keep up; he enunciates, ploddingly: "Saint Pee-tar and Saint *Pole*"; the money entrusted to him for the poor he keeps for himself; and he uses his elderly parents as domestic servants. I should also include the marvelous and absolutely unexampled detail that, in order to please the shopkeepers of his parish, he insists the needy show their invoices paid in full before agreeing to grant them absolution.

It goes without saying that, with such a topic on hand, I wasn't about to miss the opportunity to reveal that I was the author of an autobiography entitled *The Ungrateful Beggar*, that I lived exclusively upon the charity of others, and that I could not even conceive of another way of living—as a Christian. Taking my leave of the man, I had the satisfaction of seeing him ensconced in that vessel, comfortably.

Some time later, the opportunity arose to speak with more precision and energy. This jolly priest—I was almost one of his parishioners—had felt the need to exercise his ministry in abusing a few phrases of mine, and in a rather serious way. I thought I'd been wronged and told him so in writing,

---

1. Bloy's term is *rond de cuir*, which is what these cushions were called, but the term later came to be associated with the office workers themselves. The English perjorative *pencil pusher* is roughly equivalent, but I've unrolled the metaphor for sense, and to retain Bloy's play on *rond*.

demanding he apologize to me *in my home,* unless he'd rather I address myself to his superiors, and to the newspapers after that—ultimatum with a guaranteed result.² The rogue came straightaway, not to offer me apologies but to prove he owed me none. Dug in behind his seminarian Commonplaces, he seemed invincible in his unassailable contempt: for Saintliness, for the Perfection of the Gospels, for the Word of God, for Prayer, for everything that isn't Hard Currency. From the first I felt disheartened.

Impossible to make him understand anything at all. I don't remember ever having seen such a foolish man. Oh, he made a great addition to my observations on Sacerdotal Mediocrity! Asked about the prayer of supplication, the ass had this to say: "God works no miracles except on behalf of saints." I objected immediately, citing the Gospel's ten lepers and the cures effected at Lourdes, which left him silent, his mouth hanging open like a cooked fish.

Had I not already been edified long since, the *professional* smile of this cassock, each time I presented him with another Text, would have enlightened me as to the horrible degradation of the modern clergy. It is horrifying—and comforting, when you consider that the harbingers of Upheaval must be so.

In the course of this more than comical interview, he counseled me benevolently to pursue some other vocation than that of a writer, a vocation that would "nurture my manhood." It would have been fun encouraging him to take his own advice. I abstained. But what seemed extremely significant to me was how he kept returning, quasi-automatically, to this horrified exclamation: *Hold out your hand!*

How many times—wanting at all costs for me to be a professional beggar, for I had told him of my immense confidence in God—how many times did he repeat those four words, with a sort of profound and intimate horror, thus indicating (as a way of heightening his amazement) that he supposed this to be my own habitual attitude! Such an act was obviously, to his eyes, the epitome of shamefulness and infamy, but without it, it's just about impossible to present oneself as a Friend of the Savior of the Poor. So the visit came to its inglorious conclusion. I awarded this wretch the shoddy-priest certificate he seemed to

---

2. A sketch of the episode is also described in the third volume of Bloy's *Journal* ("Quatre ans de captivité à Cochons-sur-Marne"). The entry for January 31, 1901, concludes: "Some day the messenger of the Holy Spirit will make this pronouncement, that any Christian who lacks valor is a swine. And our scandalized Pharisees will say, as in the Gospel of St. John (6:61), 'This saying is hard, and who can hear it?'" —J. P.

have come asking for, and our relationship ended there.

This unsavory recollection is fading away. And if not for my furious research of Bourgeois Expressions it would never have been reawakened. But this horror before an outstretched hand, this sacrilegious and renegade embarrassment over a gesture proper to ten thousand Saints: wasn't it an admirably, frightfully distinguishing feature of this gelding of the cloth, who in his single person exemplifies an entire world?

XCIV

RESPECT DECORUM

Respecter les Convenances.

This one's an offshoot of the Commonplace that precedes it. What could be more disrespectful of Decorum than to hold out one's hand? A first-rate boor might indulge in the most unseemly transgressions and forget—or, if you like, remember—himself to such a degree as to perform obscenities in female company that my well-known reserve forbids me from describing in further detail. If he has money, they'll beg him to make himself comfortable. However little he wants to, a rich man will never offend against Decorum. For him it would be as impossible as to enter the Kingdom of Heaven.

XCV

ACT IN GOOD FAITH

Être de bonne foi.

"I'm a man of good faith. I killed my father in good faith. I believed I was doing him a favor. I believe it still. He was tired of living, had been for a long time, and every one of our neighbors could tell you he was a hard old man to deal with.

"Put yourself in my shoes, Ladies and Gentlemen of the jury: what else could I have done? Was there any other way for me to prove my affection to him? He was the product of another century. I led a wild and dissolute life and he reprimanded me for it, not understanding that we're only human, and that you have to let youth run its course. Impossible for us to see eye to eye.

"On top of that, I needed money. It was better anyway, for him and for me, just to get it over with. Oh, he didn't suffer, give me more credit than that! I struck him down with a single blow, as humanely as possible, I'm not the sort of person who takes pleasure in causing pain. If everyone followed my example, we wouldn't be so hung up on trivialities and the cows would be safe in the pasture."[1]

---

1. "*...les vaches seraient mieux gardées.*" A reference to another French proverb, from Florian's fable, *Le vacher et le Garde-Chasse* (1793), in which a father punishes his son for having traded duties with the gamekeeper. Neither has experience in the other's competency, so both game and herd are lost—and the boy earns a thrashing from his father.

XCVI

NOT THE FIRST ONE TO COME ALONG

N'être pas le premier venu.

He's not the first one to come along. Once the patriarch of the family—that is to say, the head of an important commercial concern—has said this regarding, for example, one Monsieur Trouillot, the matter is settled. Trouillot will have the man's daughter.

The highest title, to Bourgeois eyes, is *not the first one to come along*. He would pour scorn on you, were you to tell him that Napoleon was the first one to come along. The seventy-eighth, maybe, if you insist, but the first? Never! Nor the last. The Gospel says that the last shall be first, and the Bourgeois remembers that much.

What horrifies him more than anything, is the possibility that he might indeed be the first or the last to arrive, however or whenever he may arrive, wherever he may be arriving to. What he wants to be—what he has to be—is part of the crowd, resolutely and forever more.

XCVII

SOW ONE'S WILD OATS OR
YOUTH MUST RUN ITS COURSE OR
WE'RE ONLY HUMAN

Jeter sa gourme, ou Il faut que jeunesse se passe, ou On n'est pas de bois.

A prodigal son, who never had to look after pigs himself but really could have used someone to look after him, came back to live with his parents after three years studying in Paris. There's reason to believe he'd plunged rather deeply into his studies, for he had a nice crown over his brow, a missing lip, eyes that might be taken for chrysanthemums, and four blue mushrooms blooming on his face.

I don't know whether they killed the fatted calf for him, but it's been widely said of the young man that he had been "sowing his wild oats," etc. Just the other day, the local newspaper announced the profitable marriage of this little prince to the eldest daughter of a veterinarian. It's easy to imagine the envy this pure and modest fiancée must arouse in her fellow virgins.

XCVIII

MARRY WELL

Faire un bon mariage.

In principle and generally speaking, what is known as "marrying well" consists in marrying *anyone at all*. Nothing is more easily demonstrated.

To marry someone well-known, someone who might actually be *somebody* as opposed to *anybody*, necessarily supposes a choice based upon some particular esteem for the other person. In Bourgeois jurisprudence, however, this constitutes—need I say it?—a kind of disorder that cannot be tolerated.

The first and indispensable prerequisite for marrying well is to privilege money above all other considerations, while taking great care to tell yourself that all other considerations are trivial and, therefore, full of danger.

Arithmetic is the preliminary surety, the sole prelude, the unique repetitive melody of serious people who've made up their minds to sleep together. The priest should give his blessing (if the clientele require this trifling formality) and the municipal authority should grant its more decisive sanction to human couplings as loveless as, or even much more loveless than, those of animals in heat. In this way and not some other good marriages are forged—and children born with silver spoons.

XCIX

GET IT OVER WITH

Faire une fin.

That is to say, marry well or poorly only get it done. But here the Bourgeois thinking is rather convincingly veiled, for it seems to me that marriage, however one wants to understand it, is much more a beginning than an end.

The purely philosophical sense of marriage, conceived as the *end goal* of the Bourgeois, is inadmissible. The end goal of the Bourgeois is the Bourgeois himself, and much more so than he imagines, *infinitely* more, in all likelihood, than God is the end goal for most Christians. Never was a Mexican or Papuan idol so adored as the Bourgeois adores himself, nor did any idol ever demand such frightful human sacrifices.

The monstrous Transvaal War[1] is a burnt offering to the English bourgeoisie, whose representative type, at present, appears to be the horrible manufacturer of Birmingham.[2] Shall we say that England is simply in the process of getting it over with? I give the proposition my hearty consent, but in this case we aren't talking about a marriage, and so—the Commonplace remains a mystery. To the devil with it then!

---

1. i.e., the Boer War.

2. Likely a reference to Joseph Chamberlain, who made his fortune manufacturing screws before entering British politics. He held the post of Colonial Secretary during the Boer War.

C

MAKE ONE'S PEACE WITH IT

Se faire une raison.

The verb *faire*–to do, or to make—is one of the most difficult in the French language, especially when used pronominally or *reflexively,* as the good grammarians say. If you want to form an idea of the potential abyss between two of its innumerable meanings, tell yourself that a man busy shaving (*se faire la barbe*) can, at the same time, "make his peace with it" (*se faire une raison*). I hasten to point out that, while any man can shave his own face, the ability to make one's peace with anything is the province of the Bourgeois alone.

So here we have another tricky one! I know well how little clarity is to be hoped for generally from the confrontation of these Commonplaces with their ordinarily accepted meaning. Those meanings, ever outstripped, remain earthbound, at an incalculable distance from the true sense one might imagine coasting through the heavens. Let's give it a shot nonetheless.

Ernest Mijoton, second assistant to the assistant law clerk, had been waiting for his mistress for five quarters of an hour. It was coming down cats and dogs,[1] as we connoisseurs of the Commonplace like to say. It seems that waiting, even for the most delicious creature, with a frozen nose and one's feet in the mud, is more than courage can bear. In his mind he retraced the *petitions* and *arguments* whose drafting had so charmed the course of his day, but even this couldn't dispel the fact that the current proceedings gave neither him, nor his heart, any joy. No, this standing around in the soup left him extremely depressed.

His love life wasn't going so well. Eléonore strung him along with remarkable casualness. Two nights ago she'd made him hang around for two and a half hours, and when at last she arrived, she furtively squeezed his hand and then instantly, mysteriously, took leave of him again. A week earlier, for having exposed a particularly impudent lie of hers, she broke his umbrella over his head, right in the middle of a fancy café, thus topping off a barrage of insults. They were both thrown out of the place, drenched in shame.

In short, he should have ended it twenty times by now, but no matter his

---

1. Another use of *faire:* "il faisait un chien de temps…"

rage he could never get further than a few vague professions of independence. All the enchanting girl had to do was call him her "great big dodo bird," and once again he would find himself instantaneously and inextricably bound. Besides, he was a decent guy.

On the evening in question, he waited in vain for close to four hours and, despite having caught a terrible cold, didn't abandon his post until the last stroke of midnight, telling himself (in keeping with his changeless habit of twenty odd years) that he simply had no choice but to make his peace with it.

This story's on the verge of becoming tedious, so I'll expedite the rest in a few short words. After living like this for several more months, the all too faithful Mijoton had to be committed to a mental institution. Did he ever manage, finally, to *make his peace with it?* Who can say? But it was an idiotic way to end up, and he didn't go unmourned.

CI

SET UP SHOP

Monter une affaire.

You might as well say set up a swindle. Or set someone up for a sucker. The best business in the world would be to subdivide or sell the Garden of Eden, based on a roll of the dice. There'd be money to be made in that, if the embryonic state of our geographical knowledge weren't so unshakably opposed to it. Luckily, this place of delights remains hidden—well hidden and well guarded. All signs indicate that, ten thousand years from now, the first bourgeois granted entry there will still have yet to be born.

Try to look this horror directly in the face: the exploitation and carving up of the Garden of Eden; the sudden entrance of notaries, surveyors, entrepreneurs, and electric trolley lines beneath this six-thousand year old canopy which bore witness to human Innocence…!

The Bourgeois hates paradise and does what he can to destroy it, that is his nature. No sooner does he notice some beautiful Property than he dreams of cutting down its trees, drying up its springs, marking out roadways for it, installing storefronts and public urinals. He calls this *setting up shop*. I've been assured there exists on Golgotha a reasonably priced convenience store.

CII

SUPPORT THE ARTS

Encourager les beaux-arts.

When, in his retirement, the Bourgeois has married away his last daughter, he turns his support to the arts. That and stamp-collecting, you can set your watch by it. This precious support consists in paying an exorbitant price for the leftovers—or the very cream—of decorated artists. Between Memling[1] who is still unknown and some dauber from Luxembourg he won't give a second's hesitation. Try to interest him in the canvas of a young genius not yet engraved on the sacred tablets of Artists Under Commission, and he'll tell you he doesn't like to encourage "crapulence."

He has an unbelievable nose for sniffing out the laborers-at-nullity, the cretins of popular success, the debasers and demeaners of art. These last are especially dear to him. They give him so exactly what he needs! His private thirst, his profound desire, his personal crusade, is to lay Beauty *low*, lower than the foulest filth, and nothing quite scratches that itch like a sty of artistic swine.

If Enthusiasm didn't shriek like a skinned rhinoceros when you try to bring it into a brothel, you'd need that word to express the sort of supernatural agitation we're talking about here.

---

1. Hans Memling (d. 1494), German painter working in the Early Netherlandish tradition.

CIII

FROM ARGUMENT SPRINGS ENLIGHTENMENT
De la discussion jaillit la lumière.

From among the populace spring primarily fisticuffs, and in that case the enlightenment could only be an allusion (a rather heavy-handed one) to the thirty-six candles mentioned above.[1] Among the Bourgeois, however, that's not how it goes. Step into a local café some time, one of those good old cafés full of workers or shopkeepers where everybody knows everybody else, where the always affable proprietor shakes every client by the hand, where the apparition of a stranger gives rise to moldy remarks on the Franco-Russian Alliance. Not twenty minutes will have gone by, and you're sure to be bearing witness to an argument over a hand of Manille, or a contested point in a game of billiards, or some other terribly thrilling affair.

Then you'll see the light begin, very gradually, to appear. Maybe this light—or *lumen rectis*, as the Prophet King put it—won't shine, strictly speaking, on the point of contention, but at least it will illuminate, or partially illuminate, the litigants themselves.

You'll learn that the manager of the boarding house went bankrupt during MacMahon's presidency; that the fat merchant who sells silage, grain, and refuse, is the purveyor by official appointment of the bran basket for the guillotine; that the baker spent "the best years of his life" in a penal colony; that, finally, the inspector of the registry, a profoundly corrupt man who's perfectly up to speed on his mother-in-law's conduct, at the same time passes for being something like the uncle or nephew, by marriage, of his own wife; and so on, and so forth.

All will be revealed to you—with one unique exception. You will not understand how these honest gents, far from coming to blows with one another, calmly return to their cards or backgammon the instant the argument is over. The thing is, they've obtained their springing enlightenment, and it would be unreasonable to carry on a shouting match that had no further purpose.

---

1. See note to LXXXVII.

CIV

THERE ARE TWO SIDES TO EVERY STORY

Qui n'entend qu'une cloche n'entend qu'un son.

Or, as the French saying goes, "If you only ever hear one bell, you'll only ever hear one sound." It seems puerile to conclude from this that, for example, listening to a dozen bells, you would therefore hear a dozen different sounds, each clashing with every other, but in fact that's exactly what the Bourgeois means.

What he needs, deep down, are contradictory bells, bells in cacophonous chorus, muted bells that don't even hear themselves. The supernatural harmony of our chiming church bells exasperates and cretinizes the Bourgeois. Watch him some time on a feast day, when the bells ring out full peal. You will feel, you will *see,* the presence of a beast within him, wincing and writhing about. Within this man's bowels, the *blessed* bells are going to touch upon who knows what mysterious, anarchic cravings. For such is the secret of the Bourgeois: he is an anarchist, mysteriously—in his depths.

Which explains his aversion to bells, which can only be consecrated by a Bishop, the herald and delineator of divine Unity. A *unique* bell, a *unique* sound, telling only *one* story, would give too much the impression of having been sent from heaven—and this is what gives them their frightening power.

CV

THE SUN SHINES ON US ALL

Le soleil luit pour tout le monde.

More or less. But that goes without saying. Certainly it doesn't shine so brightly upon Greenlanders as on the inhabitants of the Sunda Islands. It's also inarguable that the light of this star is more dazzling to the clear-sighted than to the blind.

I'm sorry to say it, but this Expression rather lacks exactitude. It has neither the elegant bearing nor the lofty style of so many others we've already mentioned. It seems to me to derive—forgive my irreverence—from cobbler-speak, like the celebrated Rights of Man it claims to allegorize. Rest assured, whenever you hear it, there's an honorable citizen in your vicinity, eager to cast you out and take your place. It has an equivalent in the famous slogan of expropriation: Out of the way so I can take your place.[1] But who knows what the sun has to do with any of this.

And there you have the mystery of these Expressions. For going on ten years now, I feel a sort of terror whenever I hear this one. No sooner is it pronounced than I see a horrible fellow, a usurer I've met before who was blind like Homer: his dirty hands were worth a dozen eyes, and groping about he would pick your pockets with such alacrity, such subtlety, such sureness and competence as have never seen their equal.

I don't know why, but he had a great fondness for this Expression, which he repeated every other minute, imputing to it, I imagine, some form of mesmeric power. It was terrifying to behold, I assure you, the face of this confederate of darkness, going on about the glorious Sun while seeming to stare at you, into you, with his two white eyes.

---

1. *"Ôte-toi de là que je m'y mette."*

CVI

IF WE ALL JUST PUT OUR HEADS TOGETHER...

Tout le monde a plus d'esprit que Voltaire.

When will we get around to organizing a prize of two hundred thousand francs for the clever chap who can tell us who this "we all" is? I don't suppose I'd win anything myself. After all, seen from above (and not very high above), Voltaire looks to me to be about as stupid as "we all" are—which doesn't shed much light on the enigmatic turn of phrase.

In his capacity as universal suffragan, the Bourgeois must believe this Commonplace flatters Voltaire,[1] since it implies that, in order to lump together more brain power than that patriarch of wicked imbeciles could muster on his own, we would require no less than the entire mass, the totality of *all* men and women.

But the sophism here is too obvious. What the Bourgeois is asking for is a level, nothing more. *All* of us? Why that's *him*, and will be him, indefinitely, level with the muck! And he is perfectly right to imagine Voltaire lower than he. Voltaire is the orifice his excrement passes through.

---

1. The French expression answers the conditional with "...we'd be smarter than Voltaire."

CVII

THAT WHICH PROVES TOO MUCH, PROVES NOTHING

Qui veut trop prouver ne prouve rien.

Watch out now. Say I want to prove, by honest means, a geometric theory, an historical fact, an assertion of moral theology, what have you. When should I call my proof to a halt then? At what point precisely?

I'd always believed that either you proved something or you didn't. Now all of a sudden I learn that you can prove *too much*. This flips all of my ideas right on their heads. You can eat too much, drink too much, that's perfectly understandable. You can be too much of an idiot or too much of a pig, that's plain to see. It even appears you can be too honest, which is rarely a problem for the Bourgeois, equable and even-tempered man that he is. But to *prove* too much, and thereby to prove *nothing*, that's a greater marvel than I can grasp.

Let's turn our backs to the blackboard and drop our heads between our legs, in order to see the problem the other way round. Okay, I'm in position. This time I'm going to try not to prove quite enough and stop myself just a hair's breadth short of where the proof would be complete. Victory! Not having proven too much, I have at long last proved something. But alas! In the very same instant, this proof assures my doom. By its mere existence, it exists *fully*. The hair's breadth has therefore been crossed. Despite my precautions, I have proven too much and so it follows I have proven nothing at all. Impossible to escape this circle, where all of mathematics, science, and philosophy go to die.

CVIII

IT'S NEVER TOO LATE TO SET THINGS RIGHT

Il n'est jamais trop tard pour bien faire.

Hostile little adverb, "too." Here we are again, at a loss for what to think. Could it really be that it's *never* too late? Are we to believe that at such and such time it's *rather* late, without being *too* late, and that at such and such another time it's *too early,* which would be the right time to set things wrong? And this latter moment—so critical!—when does it begin and when does it end? Must I tear myself from the arms of vice at five-thirty in the morning, in order to hurl myself into those of virtue at a quarter to six? Is that early enough, or a bit late, or even very late but without being *too* late? Would I be better off waiting till seven in the evening, or even midnight? etc.

But let's set all that aside. What are we talking about here, in substantive terms, and what are Commonplaces, finally, but Bourgeois language itself? Reflect on that a moment: *Bourgeois language itself.* Really, then, nothing could be simpler. And what could it mean to *set things right,* if not to set things in accordance with what the Bourgeois wants, what pleases him, what profits him, what he orders by his commands and nothing more?

It is quite certain, for example, that if you want to break your neck for his sake, and give him your every last possession, he'll think you're only doing your duty, a bit late perhaps, but not too late. Conversely, if he finds a way to take your money, your house, your wife, or even your skin, and if all this seems useful or agreeable to him, then you don't have the slightest say in the matter. He's setting things right as can be, *absolutely* right and at just the perfect time—which is to say, at whatever time he pleases, but never too late.

CIX

A BIRD BUILDS ITS NEST ONE STRAW AT A TIME
Petit à petit l'oiseau fait son nid.

"Bloody Bulgarian blackguard!" shouted the countess of Sainte-Périne. She was right. You will surely never meet a more hateful bastard than this particular editor-in-chief. He's unqualifiedly boorish, the absolute of Boors. It was he and none other who, receiving a great poet (now deceased) who had come to offer him a few verses—which would have done incredible honor to his otherwise somber rag—put on a show of not even turning around and volunteered what has since become a famous reply: "If you'd be so kind, dear fellow, you can put your manuscript in the wastebasket yourself."

Wonderful idea her husband had had to send her there! Though her former profession as a midwife had prepared her to handle every impulse of loutishness, this rogue welcomed her with such insolence as left her utterly suffocated. Far from overcoming his resistance—as she modestly flattered herself she would—the brute hadn't even let her get a word in edgewise. Oh, it was a business well worth *getting mixed up in.* Swollen with rage, she returned home directly.

The doctor Maurice de Sainte-Périne,[1] his wife's husband through and through and, by the effect of some mysterious process of selection, a count, was that surprising *arriviste*, well-known today and even receiving patients, who in less than ten years fell for the whole River of Shit. At the time of these events, he was only just starting out and managed rather audaciously to hitch his dinghy to a provincial midwife that some town of three thousand souls had once been proud of. Just as the sun shines a luminous bit of joy on the indigent, so did this frizzy, lustrous bronze-haired person light our medical student's way with a little course in obstetrics. They understood and supported one another, the bride still having some verve left in her, and the groom a kernel of instinct.

---

1. While the anecdote is somewhat uncertain, the person here referred to is easily identified: Maurice de Fleury, doctor of medicine and man of letters, a very close friend of Bloy's around 1880, who broke with him in 1889. The name itself is transparent; Fleury had been the resident physician at Sainte-Périne when Bloy met him. The "great poet" mentioned above was in all likelihood Villiers de L'Isle-Adam. —J. P.

The latter had come up with the scheme, which modern idiocy allowed him to carry out, at least in part: to establish a sort of literary clinic, for dining rooms or high-speed trains, by way of a periodic or occasional Epidaurian journalism.[2] The idea, to put it in clearer terms, was to slip in among the pages people were reading brief little academic emollients—like a perfidious nurse slipping cannulae into unsuspecting bums—though nothing, of course, that might offend anyone. Colorless, fluent and neutral medical gossip, rather similar to the ineffectual enemas given to homebodies. The stuff was irritating and bland, but managed to ruffle the frills of a few celebrities, happy all the same for a free dose of laudanum.

On the strength of platitudes and filth, the undeterrable Maurice managed to pass himself off as a quasi-authority, a sagacious observer, the most refined of all the stinkbugs of specialized information, and thus introduce himself into certain social slits, into the cracks and fissures of the old *boutique du Monde*. I've been told he even found a clientele, and that his wife, whose heavy dough had had time to rise in the kneading trough of their misery, was finally able to enjoy a *salon...!*

But for the time we're interested in, I repeat, all these grandeurs were yet to come. Doctor Maurice, not yet emancipated from the daily expedients of lowly domesticity, exploited his companion to burnish his own position. He was counting on Lucine for the parturition of obstructed indulgences, and for the happy delivery of long-gestating good will.

However, please don't believe I'm insinuating anything untoward. The midwife didn't bribe anybody; she drew the line at being an opinionated nag. Everyone's free to despair or dream, but there was never any talk of suicide.

"Do you know what he told me?" she cried, coming in to greet Maurice Nosebrown, Count Bootlick of the Affable Vale of Sainte-Périne. "Well, I'll tell you his exact words: 'Your husband's brand of imbecility wouldn't fit in here. We already have another bastard covering that ground, who's well-known to our readership and highly esteemed. Besides, I don't like your husband's looks—or yours, for that matter. Therefore, about-face, please, and fuck off.'"

The doctor-count has a massive nose which allows him to sniffle quite powerfully. Having thus invigorated the council of his thoughts with a generous

---

2. Perhaps something like the "Health and Wellness" sections in contemporary newspapers...

snort of air, his eyes stinging, he approached his midwife who had let herself collapse onto a chair and, kissing her forehead piously, spoke to her slowly with the inspired tone of an ancient bard:

"My poor friend! Take comfort. Doesn't our own good conscience give evidence on our behalf? We have to make our peace with it, nothing is absolute and you can't have everything. One has to be practical, don't forget, and keep pace with the times. And besides, after all, we weren't put on this earth to enjoy ourselves. Patience! Rome wasn't built in a day, true enough, but the sun shines on us all and, you know, a bird builds its nest one straw at a time…"

And, according to the poet, upon that day they read no further.[3]

---

3. Cf. Dante's *Inferno,* canto V (Paolo and Francesca): *"...quel giorno più non vi leggemmo avante."*

CX

LITTLE STREAMS FORM MIGHTY RIVERS

Les petits ruisseaux font les grandes rivières.

So says my local grocer, pocketing the spare change of the destitute. So says this or that financier, running off with the savings of humble folk. So says Chamberlain, seeing the blood of little Boer children spilled. And all three are saying the exact same thing.

CXI

HAVING BEEN, YOU CANNOT BE

On ne peut pas être et avoir été.

That's where you're mistaken, my dear Assistant Undertaker, and the proof is that having been an imbecile in the past in no way prevents you from being one still today. The opposite, in fact, is what never quite materializes. You can, therefore—in the Absolute—be *now* and have been *then* whatever you like, and the same goes for Madame your wife, you can be sure of that, no offense intended.

But God save us from rash judgments! When it comes down to it, doesn't this maxim of yours just mean, obviously enough, that you can't be young forever, at least in the biological-reproductive sense? Ah, François Coppée, dear friend, what a ray of light!

CXII

IF YOUTH BUT KNEW AND AGE WERE ABLE!

Si jeunesse savait, si vieillesse pouvait!...

Well, what would happen then? The prudent Bourgeois takes special care not to give an answer. But let's hear it, shall we, once and for all. If youth but knew, it would accomplish such depravities as old age itself remains perfectly ignorant of, and, one more time, if age were able—and let's be clear, we're talking about Bourgeois old age here—what would happen then? A hundred to one you won't be able to guess.

It would behave virtuously! and the whole face of the world would be changed. Such is the dreadful secret I've long hesitated to reveal.

CXIII

IF ONLY WE KNEW EVERYTHING!

Si on savait tout!

Then we would be God—an infinitely disagreeable situation because in that case we'd be forced to deny our own existence under pain of being taken for imbeciles; we'd have to wrangle with the Worshipful Master of Freemasons and get a bad reputation in the neighborhood. We wouldn't find anyone to lend to us on credit anymore, and no one would wave their hand at us in greeting. We'd earn a reputation for working miracles and for having a victim of crucifixion in the family. In short, we would be—we, this omniscient Bourgeois under indictment for divinity—we would be what the vile mob, devoid of philosophy and confounding Substance with Happenstance, refers to as *a sanctimonious prig.*

Oh, believe me, the surest way is not to know anything, and above all not to create something out of nothing, beginning with yourself. Moreover, isn't that the tradition? Tell me, what was that golden age when the ancestors of our bourgeoisie believed it profitable to create the moon and the stars? There are so many things we can benefit from being ignorant of, and so many others it's useful *not* to do! Besides, isn't the unique purpose of life to earn a whole shitload of money, thereby to acquire eternal Death?

CXIV

YOU CAN'T THINK OF EVERYTHING

On ne saurait penser à tout.

Let's be reasonable, shall we? I have no choice but to think of my own business first; next, of other people's business, so I can muck around in it if possible; and then, at last, of my personal entertainment. Where the hell do you expect me to find time to think of anything else?

You talk to me about God, that's very considerate of you, but seriously, what do you expect me to do with this God of yours? I don't think about Him, ever; I haven't thought about Him, ever; and I'll still be not thinking about Him, please believe me, when I'm on my deathbed. Priests say it themselves, don't they? Ashes to ashes, dust to dust. So what's the point troubling oneself with all this nonsense?

You're really too funny, pretending you're interested in my soul, as though I were interested in yours! Come now, come now! It's obvious you aren't a businessman. If you were, you would know that, far from being able to think of everything, it's more than enough—and sometimes too much—just to think about the company ledger! Really, my dear sir, what do you want me to tell you? What I'd like is a God who has a nose for business, then we'd be able to get along. And in that case, he wouldn't have time to think of everything, either. *He'd be open on Sundays,* that's for sure, and he'd leave us in peace, there's my answer for you…

Such were the remarks of the fellow who replaced the savage Genius[1] who used to shout at careless navigators back in the good old days, at the Cape of Good Hope.

---

1. A reference to the "untameable" earthborn Titan, Adamastor, whom the Portuguese poet Luís de Camões created to personify the stormy Cape of Good Hope. Telling his story to Vasco da Gama in Camões' epic poem *Os Lusíadas,* Adamastor prophesies the ruin of future vessels attempting to navigate the peninsula. —J. P.

CXV

YOU CAN'T DO TWO THINGS AT ONCE

On ne peut pas faire deux choses à la fois.

Translation into Bourgeois-ese of *Nemo potest duobus dominis servire*.[1] No one can serve two masters. Only a kind of modesty prevents his boldly citing the original Text, and the word *thing* is what gives it away. It's a bit like saying: He's got a thing going on, he's having a hard time with his thingy, or he's afraid to show his whatchamacallit. For the Bourgeois is ashamed of what is noble or beautiful, just as others are ashamed of what is hideous or unclean. The very nuance by which his genius is revealed!

The holy Word, however, even translated the same way, has no binding effect upon him. For this creature, possessed by the One called *Legion*,[2] this unwitting tenant of desert sepulchers which two thousand pigs could barely manage to dislodge, continually evades domestication whenever necessity demands.

The Bourgeois would no longer be himself if he went in the Spirit of the Lord. He'd probably concede you can't do two contrary things at once, but only when you're trying to do them both simultaneously. In all other cases it actually works quite well. Honoring thy father, for example, and throwing a packet of filth in his face, are two perfectly reconcilable acts, so long as you take care not to undertake them in the same fifteen minute period. There's the whole rub: not to do two things *at once*. Admirable way of tempering a too rigorous doctrine. All you have to do is look at the consequences, the numberless applications…

When will the Cobbler come, who will establish the Gospel definitively?

---

1. Luke 16:13. "No servant can serve two masters, etc."
2. Mark 5:9. "And he saith to him: My name is Legion, for we are many."

CXVI

ALL IN GOOD TIME

Chaque chose en son temps.

"To every thing there is a season," says Ecclesiastes, "and a time to every purpose under heaven."

A time to be born in Bethlehem, and a time to die at Golgotha;

A time to plant the Cross, and a time to pluck it up again;

A time to kill souls and a time to heal them;

A time to destroy the House of Gold, and a time to build the house of silver;[1]

A time to weep, as the Daughters of Jerusalem wept, at the passage of the bloody Christ, and a time to laugh, as the terrible Woman Clothed in Sun will laugh, on the Last Day;

A time to mourn with Our Lady of the Seven Swords, and a time to dance with the incestuous woman's prostitute daughter to obtain the Head of John the Baptist;

A time to cast away living stones and a time to gather them together again;

A time to embrace one's Beloved who comes leaping over the hills, and a time to flee the appalling embraces from which none shall be delivered;

A time to acquire everything and a time to lose everything;

A time to keep the Law of the Lord and a time to cast it off like a useless garment;

A time to rend the Veil of the temple in two, and a time to sew the Shroud of the Redeemer;

A time to keep silent beneath torrents of abuse, and a time to speak in claps of thunder;

A time for Love as strong as death and a time for Hatred as delicious as the Eucharist;

A time for war against the saints and a time for the unrevealable peace of the happy dead.

What more could a man hope for from his toil? Solomon asks.

"I expect mine to resemble the toiling of Demons, and to have my dwelling arranged within their cabins of despair." So shall the Bourgeois reply when the *time* comes for him to answer with perfect discernment.

---

1. i.e., money (*argent*), and also, of course, the currency of betrayal...

CXVII

TIME IS MONEY

Le temps, c'est de l'argent.

Right up until he gives the absolutely sure, infallible and luminous answer you've just read, the Bourgeois will never fail to observe that all these various *times* mentioned by Ecclesiastes, and which are the sum of all time, are really only a pointlessly multiplicitous collection of terms all representing MONEY. Even the time to die—especially the time to die—is money to his eyes.

Well, then, there must be a profound truth in there somewhere—*the* Truth even, because one just doesn't make those kind of mistakes! Time and money swing back and forth, the same way equal weights or values do, coming to equilibrium in the Infinite. When the Lord of worlds let himself be sold for thirty pieces of silver, he was right in the middle of Time, and concentrated it within himself in the most expressive, most stunning, most unimaginable way...

Unwittingly, and involuntarily, the words of the poor Bourgeois, more dreadful than hurricanes, tend continually toward just such a concentration.

CXVIII

MONEY HAS NO SMELL

L'argent n'a pas d'odeur.

All in all, it's pretty delightful being able to tell oneself that the glorious Flavians were no less insatiable (and no fussier) than our very own bourgeois. Vespasian, who like Vitellius could eat two thousand sesterces at every meal, didn't stick his nose up at Roman piss—whatever the masters of the universe might excrete, he was ready to make money off it.

The example has never been lost, and twentieth-century speculators like to take advantage of it. The one difference is that this family of emperors sacked Jerusalem and put eleven hundred thousand Jews to death, while today's bourgeois are forming partnerships with Israel in order to boost productivity.

"Draw me," says the beloved in the Canticle of Canticles, "we will run after thee, to the odour of thy ointments."[1]

---

1. Canticles 1:3.

CXIX

THE MORE THE MERRIER

Plus on est de fous, plus on rit.

"Something to drink!" the poor woman called out, her voice not much more than an exhalation.[1] No answer. Thinking the hour of her final agony was upon her, she tried to stir up some contrition for her sins. Later, another wardress having just passed by, she marshaled all her strength to pronounce distinctly the following words, which she imagined could not be ignored: "A glass of water, Madam, for the love of God!" But the love of God has little credit in the Public Hospital. The employee, barely looking at her, shrugged her shoulders and continued on her way. And so once again the unfortunate Geneviève was seized with despair.

She had been brought to the hospital because her complaint—a very dangerous complaint—required care which her husband, a man without means and sick himself, was unable to give her at home. She had seen him beside her there in the carriage, this great artist, devastated, the very portrait of impotent Genius, and how devastated he was! More than she could have said. She only knew there was a chasm there, and in her own distress, which was frightful, she didn't dare think of this other distress.

And then there were the children,[2] glimpsed by the window at the last minute—only glimpsed, alas!—for she knew well how impossible her departure would have been had she gone about kissing them goodbye. Poor little ones! The memory of them was like claws around her heart!

No sooner had she arrived than she was left upon a chair, in the middle of this vestibule, with no help whatsoever, with nowhere to rest her suffering head. She thought she'd find someone to take her in, a bed to stretch out on, yet her presence appeared to have gone entirely unnoticed. However many days remained to her, she would have given half of them for a glass of cool water, and the other half to lean her head against a wall.

---

1. This whole "tale" is almost certainly inspired by the experience of Madame Léon Bloy (Jeanne), who near the end of 1895 fell gravely ill and had to spend several weeks in a hospital, recovering. It was at this same time that the author's son, Pierre, died suddenly, only a few months old, while in the care of a wet nurse. —J. P.

2. i.e., Véronique and Pierre Bloy. —J. P.

It was an hour or so before the head nurse, who had probably just finished torturing some cripples or madwomen in another ward, finally deigned to pay her some attention. Before being put to bed she was made to wait, sitting on a long table with several senile old wenches lined up in front of some bowls. She was trying to down a few gulps of the government-issue crocodile broth, when a warm and swirling odor suddenly stopped her. She noticed then with horror, that her companions were jammed into seats shaped like little parapets, which functioned as barbicans and, at the same time, funnels. But this was only the beginning.

Until then she had been able to believe she still belonged to the sad crowd of wretches who at least retain, if nothing else, possession of their own bodies. So far she still had her clothing, her wifely and motherly garments, which now would disappear, not to be returned to her until she left—should it be her destiny to leave. Every day now she would rise wearing the uniform of women damned to suffer, measurelessly, without consolation: a blue dress—and what a horrible blue!—a kitchen apron—imagine that kitchen!—a white headscarf laundered by imaginations full of slime, and a white bonnet that had never encountered any kind of innocence.

The great artist's wife thought she knew what it was to suffer. Young soul that she was, she supposed everything was young, even the devil and his power. How could she have foreseen the nocturnal terrors in this asylum, or the frightful circumstance of doors locked upon thirty or forty sick people, twenty of whom were stark raving mad? Doctors tolerate, monstrously, just such a homicidal mixture, as though a directive had been passed down to relieve the Administration of its resident patients, exterminating them through fear. The details are unspeakable and would make the inferno of poets look like a cavern of hope.

Nothing would answer the cry of agony sent forth by one of these wretches, seeing a phantom wander from one bed to another in the half-light and then draw near to her—nothing except, perhaps, rising up from the deepest wells of Agony, the cries of others still more miserable than she. The attendants are too drunk to wake up, or too busy with their filth to consent to being bothered. Should some extraordinary clamor compel them to interrupt what they're doing, only then do they come running, enraged, bearing blasphemies, insults, threats, and, often enough, blows. That very first night, when Geneviève saw a madwoman leaning over her, gazing down with ghastly eyes, she was overwhelmed with terror—and for this was promised confinement to a fiendish cell where all her fortitude, perhaps even her life, would be extinguished.

At her check-up the following day she complained of the threat, and the idiotic old coward of a head doctor replied with a smile: "That's all in your head, dear lady." He didn't want to pose an obstacle to the Administration, and so off he went, making little gestures of pity. The abandoned woman realized there would be no justice for her, no help to hope for from her fellow man. She learned the same day that her husband had been stricken with paralysis and their two little children handed over to a monster. There's no knowing what God may ask of certain souls.

She lived on, as did so many others, though none can say how or why. With the supernatural vigor of a castaway, she threw herself upon and clung to the Christian ideal of repaying generously whatever debts were hers to pay, and rescuing from their torments those dear creatures endangered by her absence. From that moment forward, a tremendous strength was given her. Her poor soul, borne above her sufferings, contemplated without despair the vistas and outlines of hell. She could hear the maledictions, the execrations, the atrocious words that make the Invisible Ones weep, the snickering laughter that makes demons appear, the frightful profanities, the protracted sobs. She could confront the obsessive, the terrible moaning of wretched women calling out to their fathers, their husbands, their children, their dead. She became acquainted with the dragon of Madness, *weeping without shedding tears*, which resembles the prolonged howling of whimpering dogs.

What cost her the most, however, was the plumed, bawling, oracular, bourgeois Idiocy of the interns and doctors, beginning with the previously mentioned old joker, who every morning in front of the row of beds would unwind his fibrous palaver. Accustomed to the superior views of her own husband, to whose limitless contempt for medicine and the homicidal mountebanks who profit from it she was also wedded, she felt more injured by the critical blunders chipping away at her already suffering body than by any of the rest of it. The day this despicable onager, having noticed her rosary, proffered the hospital's Commonplace of choice—"It's a mystery, there's nothing to be done"—she was ashamed to belong to the same so-called human race as such an imbecile, and believed herself more defiled by his Olympian cretinism than by the loathsome gaze and concomitant brutality of the medical students.

In Mexico, and particularly around Veracruz, there is a kind of vulture whose name escapes me, whose function it is to decontaminate the city by devouring all the carrion. They perch by the thousands on rooftops and along the highest walls, watching all that falls with an unerring eye. Only rarely will a bit of trash so much as reach the ground. These birds are the object of considerable esteem. No festival worth mentioning is celebrated without them, and killing them is forbidden, subject to the severest punishments. Such is the prerogative of the sick receiving state *aid* in the hospitals and asylums of Paris. They are counted on to gobble up the old flesh and other putrified scraps the pigs don't want anymore, and which it would be indecent to offer to honest dogs.

This expedient offers the multiple advantages of diminishing the risk of bubonic plague in the various neighborhoods of Paris, remedying the problem of food waste, alleviating the fear of death among the chronically ill, and finally, and above all, flooding the secular and philanthropic pockets of the interested parties with delicious, odorless gravy. The only difference between them and the aforementioned birds of prey is that the sick enjoy far less consideration, and one is at liberty to dispatch them swiftly.

Remembering God, Geneviève was able to swallow this slop, which the house physicians blessed on a daily basis. What didn't she swallow! Even though she was extremely weak and half-dead when she arrived, she was given to remain there for several weeks, surviving trials that would have overpowered a giantess. She didn't understand, she said later, how one more-than-half demented old wardress, who had hated her from the first, hadn't succeeded in killing her.

For the existence of our bedridden invalids is absolutely at the discretion of such she-hounds—what is subject everywhere else to the rigors of criminal law is, within these institutions, entirely normal, tolerated and encouraged by the good doctors themselves, who always prefer to look the other way. It would require a special Decree, analogous to the one proclaiming the Creation of the Angels, for any human creature to escape these murderers.

A nun—but of which order?—was squatting a short distance away, a rare and terror-inducing example of decadence. Geneviève wondered what sort of community could be capable of sending a bride of Christ to such a place. This one would from time to time throw herself upon her neighbors, or on the attendants, issuing such frantic cries as would resurrect the Innocents massacred by Herod twenty centuries ago. In moments like this, the Name of God spurted out of her, like water driven up forcefully from a deep well, and you would have had to hear them to believe the foul jokes these apprentice nurses made, young lushes that they were, freshly juiced upon vomit-covered mattresses in the enthusiasm of their devilry, by shopkeepers with no other real ambition.

Another woman with short hair, not a nun but more terrifying still, believed herself to be a man, dressed herself like a man as far as possible, affected the manners of a man and made advances on the head nurse, an irresistible wench who was said to have been a call-girl around Sébastopol once upon a time.

These two wretches—the barking nun and the androgyne—could be sure of what they were dealing with. And what could be more tragic, among the grotesqueries of this sector of the Abyss where everything, even death, is mediocre?

The last vision Geneviève took with her, never to be forgotten, was that of a group of madwomen sewing white dresses for the feast of Saint Catherine which was drawing near. One of them, a sort of dainty little girl with an old woman's air about her, ran around on high heels from one room to the next, looking for ribbons she never found. When Saint Catherine's Day arrived, these grim ablutions extended further still, spreading among these restless dead, coming and going with great ceremony, unable to find their sepulchers.

For the rest of her life, Geneviève will remember—a bizarre and cruel memory, floating obstinately above a crater of sufferings—a kind of song or threnody, mournful as the mandolin of Purgatory, whose lyrics were arranged by dementia but whose refrain signified this one precise thing: lucky are those who have lost all reason, *the cause of so much suffering!*

The more the merrier.[3]

---

3. The conclusion of this entry relies on the French idiom, *plus on est* de fous, *plus on rit*. Literally, "the bigger a pack of *lunatics* we are, the more fun we'll have."

CXX

ALL THAT GLITTERS IS NOT GOLD

Tout ce qui brille n'est pas or.

The notion of brilliance is no different for the Bourgeois than the collateral notion of shininess. A bootblack's aesthetic. Take literature, for example: Paul Bourget is a brilliant writer, and still young, while the author of *Quo vadis?* is another brilliant writer, verging on radiance. Such opinions assume, however, that we've reached the summit of bourgeois intellectuality. At lower altitudes, a simple lump of fat might appear as dazzling as the *Iliad*. But that's not what we're talking about here.

What we're talking about here is gold. Not the gold of golden hearts, nor the gold the celestial Jerusalem is built of, but the gold they use to make twenty-franc coins, and which is only precious because it's worth so much money.[1] Basically, this Commonplace—like so many others—is only a sort of way of expressing the incommunicable divinity of Money. For the truth is, gold can be dull. And so the brilliance or shininess we suppose it to have doesn't even match up to a pair of boots on parade day. Money itself, sacred money, has no need to shine, and here's the proof: for a thousand francs or more you can sell drivel that isn't worth the pale blue toilet paper it's printed on.

---

1. Again the French *argent*, meaning both "money" and "silver." The double entendre plays through the rest of the paragraph.

CXXI

DON'T PLAY WITH FIRE

Il ne faut pas jouer avec le feu.

The *Book of Judges* tells how one day Samson took three hundred foxes, attached a flaming brand to the tail of each one of these animals, and turned them loose upon the Philistines' harvest.[1] Thus did the awesome Nazarene[2] play with fire. I dream sometimes of a modern Samson who would set three hundred bourgeois backsides alight and unleash them among their fellows.

I wonder, though, whether this little prank would be so amusing as all that. Who knows whether the Bourgeois, even lit up this way, wouldn't become some kind of *prophet?* For fire is both a perfectly mundane word and, at the same time, one of the most mysterious of realities. And when its presence is made known, whether in whispered tones or by the desperate clamor of alarm bells, you could fairly say that it is fire that *plays with man,* driving the most lamentable imbeciles to madness with premonitions of the divine!

---

1. Judges 15:4-5.

2. This would seem at first glance to be an error, for Samson is typically described as a *Nazirite*. There is some ambiguity in the usage, however, as in Greek the two words differ by just one letter, and it's possible Bloy viewed them as having a common referent.

CXXII

GOOD LORD

Le bon Dieu.

Do you have to have a guilty conscience to go around saying *Good Lord!?* I've tried but can't picture a martyr making use of this particular example of the rule of adjectives. Sometimes Zola himself lets out a shout of "Great God!" if one of his grazing cows comes farting or hobbling his way. But from the lips of this righteous man, it's a pious exclamation, a leaping forth of the heart, while the Good Lording of the common folk implies nary an atom of devotion.

The Good Lord of the Bourgeoisie is a kind of apprentice clerk who has yet to prove his mettle, whom the Bourgeois is reluctant to honor with his confidence. He pays him poorly and regularly displays an inclination to dismiss him, only to hire him back the very same day, should the need arise. For it goes without saying that the Good Lord is extremely fetching as shop window decorations go. You'd know that if you were running the store, or if you were involved in any other scheme that, though it may not involve selling things as such, nonetheless requires those sort of marauding aptitudes in which the Bourgeoisie takes so much pride. I wouldn't be surprised if some day a deputy of the court from the outer suburbs had me show him which of the Good Lord's commandments was addressed to my particular person.

In short, and to sum it all up, the Good Lord, so rarely and laboriously swallowed by the Bourgeois, nonetheless remains in rather high demand among his clientele, and that's worth the sacrifice of plugging one's nose and choking it down. Go into any store, He's all they talk about: "The Good Lord will help you… the Good Lord is looking out for you… the Good Lord is on our side… the Good Nondenominational Lord… the Good Lord's blessing… the Good Lord abandoned us, etc." It's true one can live fairly cheaply this way. The Good Lord is so skint he'll be more than satisfied with a crust of bread and a glass of water, and settle for the most menial jobs, without even getting to rest on the seventh day. And still, he's scolded umpteen times a day by the Demon's dearest pals—for not being worth a devil!

And if this is the same Good Lord who's going to pass judgment on the Earth one day, then I think the Bourgeois is right to scorn and insult him. Clever bugger that he is, this is how he prepares for an eternity of shocks and thrills!

CXXIII

NATURE

La Nature.

I'm mentioning this one because it reminds me of my youth. It's very much on the wane of late and is used only rarely. We've become too wise for it. Back in my day, nature still signified a heap of things. "Let nature run its course," was a common reply to just about anything, "Don't get in nature's way." Now germs are all anyone ever talks about, and nature has been replaced by a syringe. Idol for idol, I prefer the older one. It was pleasant to look at, considerably less foolish, and considerably less dangerous besides. It was adored, especially in the eighteenth century, an epoch in France when an acute sense of the ridiculous still endured. Our Bourgeois has since most certainly lost this sense. He will probably no longer say, as in the days of Jean-Jacques Rousseau, that a return to the state of nature would be ideal. Something he can't quite put his finger on has warned him that it would be somewhat imprudent to appear *in naturalibus* at his café, to turn up suddenly in the buck, right around the corner from the local precinct. But he tolerates and even solicits, among many other things, the unsavory and mythical adventures of contemporary medicine.

Nature, as the modern Bourgeois conceives it (once this stinking beast has received the semblance of an education), is a wondrous pedant and a marvel of asininity, which the brevity of life renders inexplicable. All one can do is dream of that other marvel-wonder, which is consubstantial with it, and which also goes by the name of nature—Bourgeois nature itself. You could say there's some grandiosity in it, in that respect. It would perhaps suffice to recall the *reversed* mirror-image I spoke of earlier,[1] in which the face of this last of our worldly masters is reflected by the dreadful Visage of God.

As you well know, the *a priori* philosophers, the ones with no experience cleaning out a cowshed, have all said since Calvary that human nature is a state of innocence and perfection from which we've fallen, such that Virtue or Beauty would be a return toward Paradise—exactly the opposite of what is taught among the dung-scrapers. What should we conclude about the "nature" of a hideous *legion* of millions of ghastly and cacophonous voices, insolently demanding repatriation among the swine?

---

1. See XXXIV above.

CXXIV

SCIENCE

La Science.

And here we have the *labarum* of imbeciles: Science! Before the twentieth century, medicine—to speak of but one slut at a time—had no need of science and hardly deigned to make reference to it. Since time immemorial its habit had been to squat down in the excreta of those who were sick. Now it stamps around in filth of its own.

Putrefaction was complaining about not having its own prophet. So then along came Pasteur, Pasteur with his sweet, Melibean[1] name, and Germs—sixty centuries lag of creation—finally burst forth from the void. What a revolution! With germs, everything changes. The quest for the invisible beast replaces the ancient spirit of the Crusades. Science is all we know anymore. It's all we *want* to know—science alone—and each matachin dancer lays claim to his own animalculum. Every serum, every liquid plague, all the suppurations of the dead, everything that once upon a time would leak into the depths of the sepulcher, has today been restored to the light, championed, mobilized, injected, swallowed. Rabies, tuberculosis and cholera have become aperitifs or *pousse-cafés*. The chief muzhik[2] has even just discovered an elixir to cure old age. It's just up to the parents to bless their children with forty infectious cultures as soon as they're in the crib, and transform their bodies into bogs of purulence. They have a whole batch of useful citizens over at the Pasteur Institute, all exclusively devoted to the discovery of new processes of decay.

"Yes, sir, they're given accommodations for just that purpose!" So was I told, not fifteen days ago, by the resident physician at the Place de la Concorde. "And even that illustrious poisoner, Jenner,[3] to whom contemporary Europe is indebted for his con-artistry,[4] would find no straw left to bed down on in this house..."

---

1. i.e., pastoral, after Meliboeus (see Virgil's first *Eclogue*).

2. Almost certainly an allusion to Ilya Ilyich Mechnikov, a pioneer in immunology and credited with the discovery of phagocytes. —J. P.

3. Edward Jenner, English physician and scientist who pioneered a vaccine for smallpox. —J. P.

4. The French *vacherie* plays on the fact that with his vaccine Jenner was originally setting out to ameliorate *cowpox*...

What was once the fifth of seven flaming points on the Vagabond's imperial crown,[5] divine Science has become so base even the Bourgeois thinks it's something he might attain. Must this Value be depreciated in order to give an imbecile like Zola, for instance, the audacity to fiddle with it under the gaze of a people so stripped of their dignity not a single one of them dreams of spitting in the offender's face!

How perfectly the aforementioned author portrays the dirty bathwater of the human race, this shit-crust of the centuries also known as the modern Bourgeoisie; and how it must warm his bourgeois heart, that at every turn of every soiled and indecipherable page of his vomitous novels, he invokes what he dares call Science! Go fast with science, have orgasms with science, kill with science! Science so depraved even landlords would graze upon it, so debased it would muck out the kennels of raging brutes such as horrify even the Poor!

---

5. Science (or Knowledge) is indeed the fifth of the Seven gifts of the Holy Spirit; Bloy alludes to the tongues of fire which visited the Apostles on Pentecost (Acts 2:3). —J. P.

CXXV

REASON

La Raison.

"Reason," said Malebranche, "is the wisdom of God himself"—a definition that appears ill-suited to what merchants call their *corporate name*.[1] But on the other hand, who knows?

Everything and its opposite has been claimed on behalf of Reason, but the most well-trodden opinion is that it is *the opposite of Faith*. The proof of this lies in the universal horror reasonable people have of the number *thirteen,* and their unanimous aversion for getting down to their dirty work on a Friday. I knew a spirited enemy of Christianity who would surreptitiously hang his stocking by the chimney on Christmas Eve. The Worshipful Master of his lodge, having caught wind of this odd little habit, persuaded him simply—and *reasonably*—to hang them behind the bathroom door, which is much more in keeping with the traditions of Free Thought. You'll hear no objections from me.

---

1. Playing with "reason" in the French idiom *raison sociale*...

CXXVI

CHANCE

Le Hasard.

A happy chance, a chance bestowed by *providence*, as chance would have it, as chance allowed, such and such must be left to chance, etc. Chance, therefore, is God, the proof is everywhere and in everything, and—pay careful attention now!—it is the last and only God today who still enjoys the adoration of imbeciles. If that doesn't imply one hell of a thunderbolt! All the same, you have to admit it's quite an odd sort of God whose power is only positive, who doesn't have an atom of power that's *negative*. Oh, I know, it's not very clear what I mean by that. Fortunately, I have in my hand a letter written by a madman, a lucid excerpt of which I offer you here:

"You know, my dear sir, I've given my whole life over to chance, which is what you have to do when you know you were created and brought into the world by chance and that you subsist on the will of chance alone... 'The elephant salutes him with the rising day,' said Chateaubriand.[1] From my earliest youth, I swore my virginity to chance, which, as you'll acknowledge, was quite an edifying and ingenious way of losing it. I lived, thought, acted, and loved—continually—by chance.

"My fortune was an obstacle for me, so I made haste to toss it away on games of chance. And then, once I was free, I came to know the blessing of eating and sleeping as chance saw fit. I—unlike so many other people, whose religious sense has been obliterated and who will say that you shouldn't under any circumstances give everything up to chance—I have never kept anything for myself. It would be pointless to add that I have a wife, by chance, and children who, it could be said, are truly the sons of chance.

"Well then! Shall I confess? With all that, I'm still not happy. The God I adore has no Decalogue and no Sinai. Chance obeys no Commandments. It is capable of anything, it wants everything, and it does everything, but it is against nothing, *defends* nothing. Just try saying: chance wouldn't have it,

---

1. See Chateaubriand, *The Genius of Christianity* (Baltimore: John Murphy & Co., 1884), p. 139. "There is a God. The plants of the valley and the cedars of the mountain bless his name; the insect hums his praise; *the elephant salutes him with the rising day...*"

chance wouldn't allow, an offense against chance, punished by chance—you'll never manage it. With chance transgression is impossible, sin is impossible. When you go out, live it up, that's fun enough, I don't disagree, but over time, it's exasperating..."

I'm cutting the letter off here—suddenly it becomes shockingly immodest, though it's not really possible to say why. I've only retained this final prosopopoeia, which appears to apply to the bourgeois, but whose real target I've had a rather difficult time identifying: "Oh, the swine!" he wrote. "The swine! The swine! The swine!"

CXXVII

THE DARK AGES

La nuit du Moyen Age.

Formerly, fifty years ago at most, the benightedness or, if you prefer, darkness of the Middle Ages was rigorously insisted upon in entrance exams. Any young bourgeois who doubted the opacity of that darkness would have been effectively unmarriageable.

Today, thanks to the industrial art propagated by cabaret singers, bourgeois society—appetizing as it already was—has become positively medieval. Shop windows fashioned from bottle bottoms, stalls, chests, tapestries, credenzas, crockery, and wrought iron. All of this without suffering and without breaking the bank. A junk shop owner who isn't a thug should be able to improvise a collection worthy of Du Sommerard[1] in twenty-four hours or so. These days Lampmaking and Garment production have all they need to hold their own with the artists. The work doesn't have to be done for them anymore. They find it wherever they look.

True, the night goes on in darkness, even as a lonely gaslight burns. Let's call it art—a particular kind of art, naturally, but nonetheless. People seem to have a fondness for it, and so the money keeps changing hands. If it weren't for that, how could we deny the darkness of an Age in which everyone believed in God?

---

1. Alexandre du Sommerard (1779–1842) was an archaeologist and art collector who installed a famous assembly of art objects and furnishings from the Middle Ages and the Renaissance in the Hôtel de Cluny (now the Musée de Cluny), a gothic palace which he made into his home and which after his death was given over to the state. —J. P.

CXXVIII

THE INQUISITION

L'Inquisition.

This one hasn't budged. It's in exactly the same place it was a hundred years ago. The auto-da-fés, the burnings-at-the-stake, the Sanbenitos, the brodequins, the rack, the capstans, the pincers, the stakes, the saws, files, whips, nails, burning coals and jack screws, they're all still in effect. The instrument of torture is a common and vital artifact. The gasfitter's soul and the planisher's, too, need to be persuaded that the history of the Church is one long fish fry. The Bourgeois, whatever his profession, might question whether his bill has been added up correctly, but he *knows* there were one or several religious orders established for the unique purpose of gently roasting any thinking person on the spit, or skinning them alive from head to toe.

Oh, these *thinkers*, my childhood was so well crammed, stuffed, loaded, blocked up, saturated, intoxicated with them! To the point that every priest seemed to exist amid flames and gallows, surrounded by *thinking* victims. And the most atrocious thing of all, was that the more virtuous you were, and the more you thought, the less likely you were to escape these wild beasts. Nothing but tears! Nothing but cries! Nothing but desperate howling, and, for my part, nothing but juvenile exclamations of moral certitude,[1] nothing but imprecations! All of this combined with the euphonious neighing of puberty, and I started becoming a thinker myself...

There's something so captivating about the scenery and *mise en scène* of torture that people whom you might otherwise believe situated a certain distance from the shopping district, and who weren't necessarily sequestered away in impregnable ignorance—poets like Victor Hugo and Villiers de l'Isle-Adam—have happily set sail in the old galleys of the Spanish Inquisition. Each of them has had a turn playing Torquemada.[2]

Villiers, who called himself a Catholic, was the only one to register

---

1. Bloy's original uses the word *epiphenomena* here, in the rhetorical sense, as an exclamation or commentary, putting the final point on a speech. I've made the meaning explicit in order to avoid confusion with the prevailing modern usage.

2. Hugo wrote a play, *Torquemada*, about the famous Spanish Inquisitor, which Villiers adapted into a short story, "The Lovers of Toledo." —J. P.

awareness of Pierre d'Arbuès,[3] first inquisitor of the faith in Aragon, assassinated by the Jews in 1485 at the foot of the altar, later canonized by Pope Pius IX. This saint—this martyr, even—is depicted by the author of *Les Histoires insolites*[4] in the posture of an obstinate and blood-soaked hypocrite exhorting divine love to the snap of cracking bones...

Well, what do you expect! It makes you want to kiss and hold them, weeping, the bourgeois and their bourgeois-hopeful, who venture forth into the shadow of these mountains and who, through no fault of their own perhaps, become cretins.

---

3. Saint Pedro de Arbués, a Spanish Roman Catholic priest and inquisitor, assassinated in 1485 and canonized four centuries later.
4. i.e., Villiers de l'Isle-Adam.

CXXIX
THE ST. BARTHOLOMEW'S DAY MASSACRE
La Saint-Barthélemy.

I swear, I'm an inveterate grumbler. I could agree, heroically, to observe a few (by my own lights) singular or prototypical inanities, but that's where I draw the line. Who knows whether I won't soon be forced to re-adjudicate the Revocation of the Edict of Nantes, the most honorable act of Louis XIV's entire reign, and which fully half of Europe has been braying about for the last two hundred years? And right after that, won't we have to say something about the Bastille? About Freedom of Conscience, Human Rights, Universal Suffrage, the Creative Arts, and maybe throw in Mona Lisa's mysterious smile, too, just for kicks! You know what—why not? I give up!

Confining ourselves to the St. Bartholomew's Day Massacre, which might have been one of the most charming moments in the history of France, I confess to experiencing a rather painful sort of confusion every time anyone in Denmark, or Sweden, or any of the other Protestant countries has spoken to me about it. Indeed, it is commonly said in these environs, that this festival spilled the blood of several *hundreds* of thousands of pure-hearted Calvinists in Paris alone.

"Would to God it were so!" I've exclaimed, sorrowfully, every time. Try to imagine my humiliation at having to correct these grandiose figures with their humble, all too certain counterparts! I was in a situation not unlike a pauper, who, supposed to be rich, is forced to admit his destitution. The humiliation still endures, alleviated somewhat, it's true, by the consoling certainty that today the Calvinists are enthusiastically slaughtering each other, kind as can be.

It's nonetheless hard on a Catholic, never to see the end of this irony, always to have to submit here and there, in France no less than abroad, for the past thirty-three years or so, to the derogatory vituperation of imbeciles against the (unfortunately imaginary) atrocity of some old Parisian triviality that could have been such an enormous act but which, due to an incredible conjunction of blunders, was nothing more—alas!—than a kind of *emotional* bloodletting.

CXXX

EVERY RELIGION HAS SOME GOOD IN IT

Il y a du bon dans toutes les religions.

"Dear friend, I must see you this evening. You will perhaps be forced to spend the night. We might even have to subdue someone by force. This is very serious and profoundly unconventional. Believe it or not, we're going to lay hands on no less a grandee than my *landlord,* strongly suspected of having personally burgled his own tenant, yours truly. You'll understand that in order to make the absolute most of this opportunity, I need a *witness*. Come, therefore, but not too late. It must not be known I've received any reinforcement."

When I wrote this letter, a few years ago, I was living in a secluded house near some fortifications, and I was certain indeed that my dear neighbor and landlord had been entering my cellar at night to siphon off my wine and sneak away with my charcoal. This landlord was the very same Father Edouard[1] whom I tried to portray above in my entry on "the most decent of decent people." The fact is, every villainy and fraud men are capable of was written upon his face.

My plan was divinely simple. I'd made an ostentatious show of ordering several provisions sure to tempt him, and since the door to my cellar opened onto the yard, I'd left the key in the lock as a sort of invitation. Everything was engineered so that it would be impossible for him not to go tumbling down with a crash as soon as he'd crossed the threshold. My hope then was to rush over, arriving promptly enough to shut him inside. From that instant he would have been entirely at my mercy and, threatened with the prospect of appearing before the police and the magistrate, it would have been a matter of greatest ease to draw some serious compensation out of him, not to mention advance forgiveness for several months of rent. My friend was a sturdy and altogether resourceful young fellow, and with his assistance, the plot's success was guaranteed.

Success, I hasten to add, eluded us entirely. The old buffoon came home very late, by which time our enthusiasm had weakened and we were dozing off. Awakened by his fall but thwarted by the man's incredible agility, we were

---

1. He was Bloy's landlord at Grand-Montrouge (see LI above).

mortified to see him escape, not leaving us even the shadow of a proof against him. One of us took a last-minute shot in the dark and launched a cudgel at him—it struck him in the lower kidneys, but he barely registered the blow.

"So, Monsieur Edouard," my friend asked him a few hours later, "how goes the burglary?" Father Edouard, who knew how to go deaf when necessity demanded, took the opportunity to make this extraordinary response:

"Oh, my dear fellow, *every religion has some good in it!*

Some time previously, apropos of one of my books, the great rabbi Zadoch Kahn[2] served me up this same admirable Commonplace, which appears to be the beginning of the Gospel according to Saint John—for imbeciles and evildoers.

---

2. Bloy visited the rabbi after the publication of *Le salut par les juifs*. The encounter is described in his journal entry for 24 November, 1893, and does indeed mention this commonplace. —J. P.

CXXXI

HAVE A WARPED MIND, EXAGGERATE THINGS

Avoir l'esprit faux, exagérer.

What is a warped mind? A mind that exaggerates things. What kind of mind exaggerates things? A mind that says *Yes* or *No*. (See the Gospel of Saint Matthew, 5:37.)[1]

How many times have I had occasion to observe that there is not ONE word of eternal Wisdom that does not meet, on a daily basis, its perfect refutation in the wisdom of the bourgeoisie!

---

1. "But let your speech be yea, yea: no, no: and that which is over and above those, is of evil."

CXXXII

YOU MUSTN'T TAKE TOO DARK A VIEW OF THINGS

Il ne faut pas voir les choses trop en noir.

A bit of a dark view, tolerably dark, quite dark even, if you like, but not *too* dark. Just the right amount of darkness, basically, you know what I mean. And, really, a good-natured wisdom would counsel a white- or rose-colored view. At least that's the opinion of the First Man,[1] who doesn't want to warn dying people about death "even if they desire to know." No, anything but that—absolutely anything. Better to be in a coma, as far as he's concerned, than prepare oneself to die, and nothing causes him such singular revulsion as the "appalling custom" of extreme unction.

I read these things in *Le Journal*, in a column perfectly suited (I might add) to its surroundings, the late Fernand's[2] broadsheet geared toward a readership happily delivered from "the cruel requirements of faith." The First Man, in this instance, spends a lot of words on pity. Here is the final sentence, worth citing in its entirety, for I felt it evoked—prophetically—the audience of crocodiles and savage apes which the definitively liberated conscience of the Twentieth Century prepares for its citizenry *in extremis*.

"Let us educate ourselves in the practice of pity, gentleness, and compassion, even if it means shielding the sick person's bedside from signs of fast-approaching death. Let us become accustomed *not so much to devotion as to the* BENEFICENT POLITENESS that from each of us wards off useless pain and superfluous sorrow."

It's obvious that, "the health of one's soul being no longer the essential thing," the height of such politeness would consist in dispatching our sick friends *subito*, since this would surely spare them the throes and sufferings of

---

1. The reference here is to Paul Adam, whose column in *Le Journal* Bloy had just read. In his own diary entry of 21 November 1901, L. B. noted that Adam's column had inspired his commentary on this commonplace. "Most bourgeois die without receiving confession, because it would require them to do *penance*, a necessary consequence that horrifies 'honest folk' more than anyone. That's the deeper cause, and priests know this full well. In such cases the gospel story of the young rich man may be strictly applied to the dying. *Abiit tristis*—he went away sorrowful. A detestable article from Paul Adam made me think of this." —J. P.

2. Fernand Xau, journalist and founder of *Le Journal*, died in 1899. —J. P.

dying. The ancients had already discovered as much, several centuries before the Christian era.

Speaking now only of that degree of politeness that consists in letting the dying believe they might yet be cured, does the First Man know this custom is practiced religiously, and can he guess why? Had he the benefit of knowing the pastor of some parish or other, this superfluous minister could apprise him of the fact that most bourgeois folk die without receiving confession *because it would require them to do penance*. The dying man's family, fearing such a conclusion to an existence full of mischief and banditry, puts the strictest guard up around him, in order that he not "take too dark a view of things." However much he may have been asked for, the priest isn't brought in until his priestly office has become pointless and to that end, it would seem, even the most sacrilegious lies are permissible.

I'd be curious to know who ought to be the beneficiary of the First Man's compassion in such a case, because there are basically three legal persons present here, each worthy of interest: the dying man, the dying man's heirs, and the victims of the dying man's thievery. A choice absolutely must be made. If you hide from the thief the fact that he's about to die, it's not as though he'll give a thought to making things right. If you make him aware, it's still unlikely he'll give any thought to it, even after the priest's exhortations—but at least there's a chance. Not to put too fine a point on it, but this will be a hell of a business. Once again: upon whom shall the First Man's merciful pity fall?

I just mentioned[3] how the Bourgeois inflicts his ongoing refutations upon the sacred Word. The same thing, on his deathbed, makes me think—it's just that suggestive!—of the young man in the Gospel who, having asked Jesus what was required of him in order to have eternal life, received the reply that he should give everything he has to the poor. And the young man went away sad. *Abiit tristis.*[4]

Post-scriptum. The Gospel does not say *too* sad—*nimis tristis*—but only "sad," not excessively so. The Bourgeois can do without eternal life. It's what distinguishes him from the beasts.

---

3. i.e, in CXXXI above.
4. Matthew 19:22.

CXXXIII

EVERY CLOUD HAS A SILVER LINING

À quelque chose malheur est bon.

As long as the cloud is over somebody else's head, of course. In fact, that's the only silver lining there is. It's rather difficult to imagine how to take advantage of a stroke of good fortune if, for example, it lands on your neighbor out in the boonies. The proof is that one man's silver lining is another man's cloud, as expressed so precisely by another, almost identical Commonplace.[1]

Say your best friend just unexpectedly inherited several hundred million francs. Well, now! You probably won't see a penny of it yourself—and he might even try to take *your* last penny. After all, you two are like as brothers.

The most incontestably silver of linings is to see your neighbor suffer, to know that he is suffering. It's a good in and of itself, and it's good in its consequences, too—for a man struck down is a man who can be eaten. Indeed, it's a well known fact: there is no flesh, not even pig flesh, so flavorful as this.

---

1. *Le bonheur des uns ne fait pas le bonheur des autres.* One man's misery is another man's fortune.

CXXXIV

ALL GOOD THINGS TO THOSE WHO WAIT

Tout vient à point à qui sait attendre.

A Christian family. The father receives the choicest portion. *Without touching it*, the father offers it to the mother. The mother gives it to the children, who give it to a poor man, who throws it to the dogs.

Dogs know how to wait for the Body of Our Lord Jesus Christ.

CXXXV

HEALTH COMES FIRST

La santé avant tout.

What's that? First? Before money even? Oh, yes, my child, before everything, absolutely. Go easy on your mortal coil, it's the most precious thing you have and it's something that can't be replaced. Make it last as long as possible, and get all the pleasure you can out of it. The body has its needs and life is short. Priests can go on all they want about eternal life, but take it from an old man with experience under his belt: a bird in the hand is worth two in the bush and you'll be much cheerier paying the cook than the pharmacist. As far as money is concerned, you don't lose any by taking care of yourself—on the contrary. You have to know when it's time to let things idle. You'll only make up for it and then some with the clientele.

Napoleon used to say that good health is indispensable to a general. Well now, tell me, what is commerce if not a kind of war? Everyone who sets foot in our shop is an enemy. "Know your enemy," said Gambetta. "The customer!" And don't ever forget it, my son. True commercial enterprise, commercial enterprise properly understood, the kind that leads to fortune and glory, consists in selling something for twenty francs that cost only fifty centimes, just like the most respectable apothecaries do. True, it's easy for them, since their merchandise isn't subject to vulgar supervision. Nevertheless, that's the ideal.

You know as well as I do that, where food-selling is concerned, for example, the first thing you have to learn, the *basic principle* of the profession, is to serve up only garbage, taking care always to do the weighing in the darkest corner (as if I even need to say it), and with extremely quick movements, such that the customer has absolutely no idea what he's buying, either in terms of quantity or quality.

I worked some time ago for the famous Gibier, of Caverne and Gibier, generally regarded as the Massena or Cambronne[1] of green-grocers. I will remember for the rest of my life the truly heroic physiognomy and austere simplicity of that old geezer when he used to tell us:

---

1. André Masséna (1758–1817) and Pierre Cambronne (1770–1842), storied military commanders during the French Revolutionary and Napoleonic Wars.

"My friends, know this, I have never sold anything but shit! And always with my thumb on the scale, especially when selling to poor people who don't have scales at home. As far as change goes, I can testify on my own behalf that I've always found a way to pass off counterfeit coins. I've even managed, in the heat of a particularly busy moment, to slip in a few underwear buttons. But to do that you must be in good health, you have to have an iron constitution, for you must be working away, constantly, never taking a day off, never turning your nose up at a profit, however marginal, even if you've already got fifty million in the bank."

Meditate on these heroic words, my dear child, and once again, take good care of that carcass. Health comes first.

CXXXVI

GOD IS DONE PERFORMING MIRACLES

Dieu ne fait plus de miracles.

This is a benign, conciliatory, quasi-pious way of saying that He never performed any in the first place. It's the favored Commonplace of Abbé Pucelle and so many other devoted ecclesiastics and laymen of the Church!

One day, about ten years ago, I was introduced to a gentleman who, learning my name, immediately took it upon himself to astonish me; he considered it puerile, he declared, to wait around or hope for the advent of great things, or even simply uncommon things.

"For my part," he added, "I can attest that nothing extraordinary has ever happened to me."

The enormity of this foolishness paralyzed me for a moment, after which I presented him, gently, with this objection:

"Sir, you must either be extremely oblivious or extremely ungrateful, since you seem to have chosen to say this to me precisely at a moment when something amazing, something you never would have foreseen or hoped for, is happening to you."

"And what is that?" asked the man, surprised.

"You," I replied, with great simplicity, turning my back on the imbecile, "have just had the honor of meeting me."

CXXXVII

I'M NO MORE FOOLISH THAN THE NEXT PERSON

Je ne suis pas plus bête qu'un autre.

Therefore I possess an intelligence at least the equal of anyone else's. This conclusion doesn't appear altogether rigorous, but when it comes to the logic of the bourgeois, as with certain grammatical laws, *usage* is the sole determining factor. If the old umbrella merchant said to the young telegraphist, "I'm no more foolish than the next person, and the *proof* is that I've been around since before you were born," you can be certain neither stationer nor clog-maker would fail to proclaim the obvious.

The strength of a man who can affirm in good conscience that he's no more foolish than the next person is incalculable. There's so much mystery in this devilish Expression, one is almost tempted to believe it played some not insignificant role in the creation of the world.

Have your doctor, your dentist, your funeral director, your taxidermist, your notary, read some magnificent phrase from Barbey d'Aurevilly or Villiers de l'Isle-Adam, an ingenious reflection from Ernest Hello, a lively stanza from Paul Verlaine—what will these men reply, do you suppose? Simply: "We don't understand. Even so, we're no more foolish than the next person." And in that very instant, though even an angel would be unable to say why, Verlaine, Hello, Villiers, Barbey, and indeed Napoleon, if you like, together with all the great figures of history, will appear beneath their feet…

I know of nothing more crushing than the universal superiority of someone no more foolish than the next person.

CXXXVIII

TO WILL THE ENDS IS TO WILL THE MEANS
AND EVERY PENNY COUNTS

Qui veut la fin veut les moyens et *Il n'y a pas de petites économies.*

Madame and Monsieur Dog had a compelling interest in their child's death, but I no longer know why. Maybe I never knew. It was such a long time ago! I was twenty years old at the most and I've never understood anything about financial scheming or the funny business notaries get up to. I only know that after the burial of little Dog his parents were supposed to have "entered into the enjoyment" of a handsome sum. It must be said, in fairness to the parents, that as soon as this aforementioned interest found a place in their lives, they dreamed only of the means by which to find *another place* for their poor child. It would be rash to conclude, however, that the Dogs were mongrels. They were bourgeois, that's all, just bourgeois, and they passed quite properly for right honest folk. They loathed the sight of clouds on their day off—that should tell you everything.

The husband had a decent post at City Hall, and the wife ran a reading room, or a restroom, I can't remember exactly which. Both one and the other belonged, moreover, to the class of right-thinking people. They would have had serious misgivings about missing Sunday mass, and they were patrons of charitable organizations. It was said of them, respectfully: "They have this and that, not to mention their *prospects.*" What prospects? Why, the death of little Dog! And they were envied for it even as they were pitied.

"Poor Dogs! All the same, it must be upsetting for them to have this pup who would be so happy to be reunited with the Good Lord!" That was the conventional wisdom.

They had a very determined advocate in the person of Minet, the potbellied ironmonger and neighborhood oracle. "Oh, if only I were in their shoes!" he barked from time to time. He never followed through, but the gesture he made with his hand, folded at a right angle in the direction of the floor and cutting the air from left to right across his chest, underlined rather clearly the simultaneous wink in his eye, which said more than words.

The pastor himself, saccharine author of a book on *The Purity of Intention,* consoled them with love, exhorted them to bear their cross right up until God saw fit to remove the burden. In short, they enjoyed universal sympathy, and when word of little Dog's death began to spread, the whole neighborhood felt as though a weight had been lifted.

No, his parents hadn't killed him. They'd made him *live quickly,* nothing more. Were they to blame for the fact that children don't have the endurance of Tartarian camels? This one was hardly five years old, and they forced him to walk up to ten hours a day, to keep his health up. The food he ate was invariably succulent, in quantities proportionate to this salutary exercise. Never was a child more well-nourished. As for sleep, they worked it out so he didn't abuse it. Since it had been decided he would have a career in the army, they were already preparing him for that, sounding the alarms multiple times a night. And so forth, and so on.

Within a few months, the future soldier had been dispatched. Someone who sees through walls told me that when these two monsters were alone with their victim, they would take off their masks—and it was something horrific to behold. Poor little creature with no one to stand in his defense! The details can't be written down… It's common knowledge that the teardrops of the powerless are, for the bourgeois, like wine from God's own Vineyard…

Murdered by exhaustion, indigestion, insomnia, mute with terror and unable to move, the pitiful child of the Dogs went down to death, making no more noise than a little man-shaped plumb, following its line to sound the bottom of a lake.

This frightful story sticks in my mind because it is exact, *universal,* and profoundly typical. There was a particular little element of stinginess on display at the funeral, too diabolical that I should dare recount it here, but which astonished everyone in attendance.

An old plasterworker was trying to express his admiration to the happy mother. Her humble reply: "Every penny counts."

CXXXIX

MAKE THE BEST OF A BAD SITUATION

Faire contre mauvaise fortune bon coeur.

If you want my opinion, it's quite simple. In business, when we're unable to meet our financial obligations, that's what we call a bad situation. And if we can't find any expedient and have to get the hell out, we call that "making the best of it."

We use these sorts of expressions because, after all, we still have a bit of poetry left in us. But in cases where the merchant's wife has to save the outlay by putting her own body up as collateral—and in business such a possibility must always be allowed for—well, there's something to be made, but surely not *the best of it*. You get my meaning.

CXL

HAVE ONE'S HEART IN THE RIGHT PLACE
Avoir du coeur, un bon coeur.

A virgin who runs wild in order to feed her aging parents certainly has her heart in the right place. Another who runs wild in order to support a noble young man indisputably has her heart in the right place. A third who doesn't run wild at all and wants to marry a poor man has her heart in a place that is radically *wrong*. See *Les Demoiselles de Bienfilâtre*.[1]

---

1. One of Villiers de l'Isle-Adam's *Contes cruels*.

CXLI

HAVE SOME SELF-RESPECT

Avoir de l'amour-propre

The head clerk's wife has some self-respect, and the resident caretaker has *his* self-respect, but these are two cuts of the same gem.

"I'm stepping outside myself never to return," said Saint Catherine of Genoa one day, and it remains one of the greatest phrases ever uttered.

Self-respect consists in feeling *at home* wherever you are. It has been noted that decent people go out more rarely than murderers. Between these two types, that's the only substantial difference.

CXLII

A CUSHY JOB

Avoir le travail facile.

It's the *nec plus ultra*, is what it is, the supreme echelon in the intellectual hierarchy of the bourgeois. Notaries and mattress makers think that a man, in order to be truly great, must have a cushy job. A writer of genius, who toils at the brink of death for several years over three or four hundred pages, is for them the very incarnation of shameful impotence.

Between the ages of twenty and twenty-five, I listened, furious, to the way people spoke of Alexandre Dumas *père,* who back then was still an interminable shower of lukewarm mucus which two generations of woodcarvers took to be the breaking open or bursting through of cataracts of light. "Now *there's* a fellow with a cushy job!" they would say, summing up and evaluating this negro's two or three hundred volumes.

Today there's a new crop with a reputation for having an easy go of it but who suffer incredible difficulty expelling their phlegms and catarrhs. It's troubling to think that no less a polygraph than Paul Bourget, whose writings are like a diarrhea of fish glue, is nonetheless one of our most stubbornly constipated scribblers.

We could give a hundred more examples, but let's not. The more than peculiar situation for a multitude of literary types is that cushy work is the death of them. Must we conclude the same holds true for other contemporaneous cohorts? Am I to believe that my grocer, for example, fat imbecile that he is and lorded over by the nagging-est imaginable cow of a woman, has to go to back-breaking lengths, sweating blood and water, in order to finagle a few extra coins out of me?

CXLIII

SOME PEOPLE HAVE ALL THE LUCK

Avoir de la chance.

It's commonly said that a French citizen is lucky to have a father who was born before he was. It's assumed, of course, I hardly need point this out, that such a father would be a man of means. That's as lucky as it gets (and anything else would be a jinx).

In general, being lucky consists in *catching as little blame as possible*. Belonging, in other words, to that tiny number of people who manage to avoid the floggings and ass-kickings the rest of us seem to deserve. By the same token, it's certain that, to Bourgeois eyes, poring over world history from such heights as we are by now familiar with, Noah the Patriarch had *all the luck*. Here the language rises to the level of the thought.

Anyway, it's a matter of indifference that the word "luck" might be absolutely and forever unintelligible. The main thing is that it suspends the notion of Justice, or keeps it at a safe distance. Which is all that we ask it to do.

CXLIV

HAVE A LOT ON ONE'S PLATE

Avoir du pain sur la planche.

You ordinarily hear this one from individuals who are "rolling in it" and who enjoy a life of what is called "honest leisure," from the 15-franc annuity afforded to yours truly,[1] all the way up to the millions in revenue that certain others possess, raked in once upon a time by a holy ancestor, a Calvinist or Lutheran, through the blood of disemboweled Catholics. Such are the origins of great Protestant fortunes.

But most of the time, this *lot* on one's plate doesn't offer much benefit, especially not for poor people. Strange bread, it's still edible when only a few crumbs are left; when there's *too much* of it, however, it can't be eaten at all but turns to stone. The Protomartyr[2] was stoned with just such bread: the bourgeoisie of Jerusalem had a lot on their plate.

---

1. See Bloy's journal, *Quatre ans de captivité à Cochons-sur-Marne,* p. 74, December 4, 1900. Bloy had just learned, on a visit to the Caisse des Dépots et Consignations in Paris, that a "wretched bit of work for the Northern Railroad" 23 years prior would entitle him to an annuity of 15 francs beginning in 1901. —J. P.

2. Saint Stephen, the first Catholic martyr, whose death in Jerusalem by stoning was witnessed (before his conversion) by St. Paul. —J. P.

CXLV

LIVE EXTRAVAGANTLY[1]

Entretenir des danseuses.

I'd forgotten this one until just this very minute—how can that be? I've heard it so often it doesn't even register anymore. It's like the eternal "Good day, sir" of the first person to come along, which, over time, becomes impossible to hear. Just imagine, for at least a hundred years there hasn't been a single poet or artist worthy of notice who didn't live extravagantly throughout his adolescence and for however long his none-too-rigorous studies lasted.

Anyone working behind the counter, especially in the provinces, knows that a painter's studies, for example, are nothing but a gigantic farce. As for a poet's literary beginnings, those are something quite different, and a person should take care not to make allusion to them in the presence of young girls.

Oh the absurdities of my youth! Oh the extravagances, oh the dancers I indulged in then, in the gleam of my twenty years! But what of that? Don't they all, in their retail shops, or on the methodically swollen seat cushions of their government offices, don't they know that I *continue* to live this way? As always, the Bourgeois sees clearly what's going on.

One point remains cloudy nonetheless. Where in the devil do these dissolute artists go to find their dancers? Such a constant and incomparable orgy implies an infinite source of extravagance. Alas, an overly simplistic explanation can only aggravate the sad case of our poets.

These dancers are really only *one* dancer, and it's been the same dancer now for generations. Her eyes are like lanterns hung in caves, she has a leaden tinge to her complexion, a deathly pallor to her face, her fingers clenched around her withered throat, and, if you really want to know, she dances an extravagant *belly* dance in front of graveyard cafés...[2]

---

1. The French idiom, *entretenir une danseuse,* translates literally as "Keep company with a dancer," and can refer either to having an expensive mistress or, more generally, to spending one's resources on unprofitable or otherwise foolhardy ventures or indulgences.

2. *...elle danse... devant les buffets des cimetières...* This used to be a fairly common expression, describing someone who didn't have anything to eat and so would "dance" back and forth before a restaurant or café window, where food was typically displayed. The implication here is fairly straightforward.

CXLVI

IF YOU DON'T SHOW UP, YOU'VE NO RIGHT TO COMPLAIN

Les absents ont toujours tort.

Which means, as I believe everyone is fully aware, that whoever doesn't show up should invariably be swizzled, fleeced, pirated, worked over, stripped, burgled, raided, cheated, pilloried, deprived, defrauded, sold up the river, betrayed, and calumnied in every imaginable way. On that much, nobody disagrees. You might even say it's one of the essential provisions of bourgeois Jurisprudence.

There must be some deeper meaning to it, as with everything that issues from imbeciles and scoundrels. If you're curious to know who's going to suffer every insult, every iniquity, every horror of the Crucifixion, ask yourself: *Who shows up the least in this abominable world?*

CXLVII

MONEY HIDES

L'argent se cache.

"I'm going to reveal the greatest secret known to me," said an illustrious philosopher who thought himself to death. And he added, not without having taken some precautions against a sudden cataclysm: "Well, my friends, here it is: *money hides!*"[1]

---

1. Cf. Benjamin Constant, "The Liberty of the Ancients Compared with that of the Moderns."

CXLVIII

I WANT TO SLEEP SOUNDLY

Je veux dormir tranquille.

This was the landlady's final word. For her the days of struggling were over. At her age, she needed to rest easy. She had to have reliable renters, solid guarantees.

"You're absolutely right, Ma'am," answered the visitor, who'd had time to investigate the atria. "If it's up to me, you'll sleep." And off he went.

Madame Sheep was a horrid old wench who burned her money to keep warm when it was cold out. It was said she was filthy rich, and even in this atrocious petty-bourgeois suburb her avarice was legendary.

The late Ram had earned all he wanted from the exploitation of fortified milk, a product he'd invented himself and an unrivaled destroyer of little children. Snatched away too early from his spouse's tender embrace, he had gone to wait for her in an extraordinarily hideous mausoleum. It was there above a bizarre-looking entryway that I read, not without terror, these words drawn (incredibly enough) from the Gospel: *Knock, and the door will be opened to you...*

The inscription would have been out of place over the door to his widow's house. Once you'd rung the bell several times, a narrow wicket would be seen opening slowly, and within this aperture something most fantastical would appear. The old woman's frightful visage beside the ferocious muzzle of an enormous Great Dane, propped up by two paws on its mistress's shoulders. She would speak then to the newcomer with the voice of a military policeman, charged with equal parts hate and fear. If you happened to be poor, the shutter would close again violently, punctuated by some profanity. You would never manage so much as to cross the threshold without a certificate of future tenancy and a stack of references, and then you would cross a courtyard and a patch of garden with Madame Sheep and her death-hound to reach a sinister-looking pavilion.

This pavilion was a thorn in the landlord's side. She couldn't make any use of it whatsoever, and the non-value it represented caused her no end of desperation. On the other hand, neither could she resolve to take on a tenant, no matter how well they were vouched for. It was every bit as serious for her as for an honest woman to select a lover. She just hadn't ever been able to make up her mind.

In truth, she was morbidly afraid of having a stranger put up so close to her. She was a classic miser, the genuine article, the kind that adores shiny metal, kisses it with rapture, suffers at being unable to eat it the way Christians eat their God in the sacrament of the Eucharist. She could be heard in the evenings locking and bolting her doors, it took her a quarter of an hour to get to them all, and she reportedly never went to bed until she'd thoroughly inspected the grounds with her dog.

Such precautions are so commonly linked to ironic catastrophe, no one will be surprised to learn that Madame Sheep was found at home one day, stabbed to death and almost decapitated. Her neighbors, used to her eccentric habits and knowing that no human being was ever authorized to set foot on her property, didn't realize any crime had taken place until quite a bit later, when the odor of the carcass had begun to spread. She was discovered in an unlit room stretched out on the floor beside her Molossus, each body in a state of advanced decomposition.

The money had been carried off in full, and the murderer—safe bet it was an artist—had left on the table a beautiful sheet of official letterhead, upon which was written in a very confident hand the following lines of a famous refrain:

Sleep, sleep, my beauty,
Sleep, sleep forevermore.[1]

---

1. Cf. Victor Hugo, "Sérénade" (1857).

CXLIX

I DON'T WANT TO DIE LIKE A DOG

Je ne veux pas mourir comme un chien.

Why should a person who lived like a pig be so intent on *not* dying like a dog? It's a valid question to put to oneself—and to others, for that matter.

In the first place, what does it mean to die like a dog? According to the authorities, it's a simple matter of leaving this fine world without receiving any of the sacraments, and going straight to the cemetery without any religious ceremony. So the Bourgeois who doesn't want to die like a dog sends for a priest, the parish pastor whenever possible, and speaks to him about the new tax on revenue, the advantages of intensive cultivation of Jerusalem artichokes, the disadvantages of mastic in the maxillaries of hippopotami, or the urgent need for aggressive reform in the obligatory teaching of Kamchatkan languages—a manifestation of Christian faith which will give him the right, after death, to have his carcass carried to the church and accompanied by a surplice all the way to the cemetery, unless his family balks at the expense.

Need I say that all this is just so much playing for the gallery? You go to your maker playing for the gallery in order not to die like a dog. Either you'll understand that or you won't, but you have the whole thing right there.

"I could give a shit about religion," says the seed merchant, "but I don't want to die like a dog."

The shop's clientele depends on it, if the clientele is made up of right-thinking people. And if, on the other hand, it isn't, well, the interests of the enterprise demand that the boss go graveward like a dog. But that's a rare case in the nicer suburbs, where we know how to have a good time.

CL

ANY FRIEND OF YOURS IS A FRIEND OF MINE

Les amis de nos amis sont nos amis.

The Chevalier du Bran d'Enhaut had saved the life of a small-time lawyer at the High Court of Normandy. When the Terror came along, this lawyer full of gratitude recommended his benefactor to a cabinet-maker, who recommended him to a cobbler, who recommended him to a cesspit cleaner, who recommended him to a defrocked Benedictine monk, who recommended him to the prophetess Catherine Théot,[1] who recommended him to Robespierre, who had his head chopped off. No good deed goes unrewarded.

---

1. Catherine Théot (1716–1794) claimed to be the new Eve and mother of the Messiah. During the Revolution, an inquiry was opened against her, which attempted to implicate Robespierre, whom she had designated as the Savior. She died in prison one month after Robespierre's execution. —J. P.

CLI

I'M SPEAKING TO YOU AS A FRIEND

C'est en ami que je vous parle.

This is how a County or Registry Office employee speaks to his closest friends, when they're in jeopardy and he's decided not to do anything about it.

A man whose landlord speaks to him "as a friend" is the most thoroughly defended, judged, and executed of men.

CLII
A BOOK TO KEEP BY ONE'S BEDSIDE
Un livre de chevet.

We're talking about the elite here. Your average bourgeois doesn't read anything at all and, consequently, keeps no book by his bedside. The only book capable of holding the interest of a novelty shop owner or wine wholesaler is the ledger book, an enormous *folio* with brass corners that one has a hard time imagining beneath a bolster pillow.

Laborers read more. Of course they only read what they can, but they read. The Store doesn't own them. They aren't directly beneath the Idol's gaze. They have permission, if only for half an hour a day, to tend to their souls, their own poor souls, and some of them take advantage of the opportunity.

Even so, let's admit that there is a bourgeois elite, a sacred elite for which we can assume at least one bedside book for each 32nd half-brigade. What on earth could this book be? Impossible for me to know. I've heard tales of certain mathematicians sleeping with the logarithmic tables, but someone must have been having one over on me, that's already too literary by half.

My guess is rather than a few old grannies out there still nod off in the arms of Paul Bourget or Maupassant, while some younger ladies of various generations guzzle down the Marquis de Sade's *Philosophie dans le Boudoir* or some other book of that genre. I have no precise data on the subject, however, and confess I don't know what to think of these much-vaunted bedside books, which nonetheless must exist, since people talk about them *ad nauseam*.

In the olden days, there was the *Imitation of Christ*—read and re-read by all. Much later, at the end of the last century, there was the *Imitation of our Lady of the Moon*, which no one, least of all me, will ever read, and whose author[1] more or less died of hunger. I've gone so far as to imagine, now and then, an *Imitation of Hanotaux*, a bedside book that remains to be written but which would require such a lack of style, such a methodical diminishment of thought, that the undertaking couldn't be proposed with any seriousness, not even to an academic.

---

1. Jules Laforgue was 26 years old in 1886 when this collection of poems was published. He died the following year—not of hunger but of tuberculosis.

CLIII

CARRY ONE'S HEART IN ONE'S HAND AND CROCODILE TEARS

Le cœur sur la main et *Les larmes de crocodile.*

It appears people can have such big hearts they have to carry them in their hands, and that, at the same time, they can wear these hearts on their sleeves, which is already a kind of mystery. One can also have heartburn and weep crocodile tears. Such astonishing physiology is characteristic of the Bourgeois, who couldn't live another day if it were taken from him.

I recall as a child being quite astonished by these hearts in hands, and I would instinctively look at a person's hand to see if it were holding one. Having understood it to be the mark of irreproachable veracity, of heroic candor and transparency, I inferred from the *absence* of this organ upon their limbs the universal dissembling of those around me. Same deal with hearts on sleeves.

Later I developed a more precise understanding. I knew exactly what to think of the bourgeois heart, and all the uses one might make of it. I daresay I reached a more satisfactory conclusion than Gargantua himself in his treatise on ass-wiping.[1] It's not a question, in this case, of carrying one's heart in one's hand, but of having the bourgeois heart *well in hand,* if you take my meaning.

As for crocodile tears, here's what I was told by an illustrious traveler, a famous lawyer from Brussels and one of the conquerors of the Belgian Congo, the last country where anyone talks about them:

"The crocodile is a boat. It doesn't exist, so to speak, as an animal, and is therefore incapable of any sort of crying. It's a mythological representation of the Poor Man who assiduously devours the Rich, those luckless victims of poverty's execrable tears…"

"Let it be known to all my people," said Our Lady of Copious Weeping, sixty-five years ago, on the dread Mountain.[2]

---

1. Cf. Chapter 13 of Rabelais' *Gargantua.*

2. A reference to the miracle of La Salette, which occurred a few months before Bloy's birth and preoccupied the writer throughout his life. c.f. Léon Bloy, *Celle qui pleure* (1908). —J. P.

CLIV

BE A SELF-MADE MAN

Être fils de ses œuvres.

Or, literally, be child to your own labors.[1] This is the worst advice the deadpan humorist known as the Bourgeois has to offer. What to make of a cesspit cleaner born of his septic tank, or a serial-writer engendered by his own serials? Is it possible even to speculate on the cosmic immensity of such a joke?

Now let's try to imagine Zola, brought forth by *Nana* or whichever other novelistic sow of his you prefer, and ask yourself: what should we think of a people that produces obstetricians and midwives for such children?

---

1. "A self-made man" is the idiomatic equivalent of someone the French would say is *fils de ses œuvres*, but the former term leans more on a metaphor of formation, while the latter (and Bloy) on a metaphor of engenderment. Liberties taken in the present translation reflect this discrepancy.

CLV
CHERCHEZ LA FEMME![1]

So cries the office worker, reading about a crime in the paper. Note that I'm speaking here of the *intellectual* office worker, the accounting clerk, for example, who makes wood-splitting gestures at you to indicate that, given the mild weather this morning, he's taken it upon himself to remove his flannel vest. This man, more far-sighted than the vulgar plebs and used to casting judgments from on high, never fails to offer this advice. His profound and altogether novel idea, which so few thinkers grasp, is that the first thing to do in any tragic affair is *look for the woman*.

I was acquainted with a very proud and very married one of these fellows, whose woman would *look for the man* as fervently as a weasel seeks a burrow. She'd find him, too, with incredible frequency and promptitude.

---

1. Literally, "Look for the woman," analogous to "follow the money." The French saying was common in English and American detective fiction throughout the 20th century, and so has been left as is.

CLVI
A RESPECTABLE WOMAN
L'honnête femme.

Once upon a time, Balzac wanted to raise Hadrian's Wall between virtuous women and respectable ones. A romantic distinction, with no exact meaning today. The two have become one and the same.[1] It's the eternal Bourgeoise of Bethlehem who refuses to shelter the Child Savior and tosses the Rosa Mystica to the north wind.

A respectable woman is one who took first prize in arithmetic when she was 14 years old and frightens the ten thousand angels which the Abbess of Ágreda[2] saw circling the Immaculate Conception.

The morose and fiery wife of the great unchained Cuckold is also a respectable woman...

O Prostitutes with no trace of falseness, for whom Jesus suffered, pitiful and holy Whores who are unashamed of the poor and who will bear witness on the Last Day, what do you think of this vile, respectable wench?

---

1. Cf. Balzac's *Physiologie du mariage:* "La femme honnête et l'honnête femme." The meaning of the adjective *honnête* is subtly altered by its placement before or after the noun it qualifies.

2. The Franciscan abbess Maria de Jesus d'Ágreda (1602–1665), whose *Mystical City of God* was reportedly dictated to her by the Blessed Virgin. —J. P.

CLVII

THE COURAGE OF YOUR CONVICTIONS

Le courage civil.

Had he merely been faced with a pack of uncharitable imbeciles, the Poet probably would have been acquitted. But the jury was drawn, as though by a demon, from a heap of storekeepers, each more honorable than the last. Hope, blown dead by the breath of Merchandise, was put to rest in a distant cemetery.

No doubt the accusation carried not even the shadow of a proof, but it was made up of such presumptions, and was supported by such a supernatural conflux of coincidences, incidents, and homicidal episodes in the course of the proceedings, that the innocent man could no longer defend himself. And then, most critically, there was the jury's obvious, ferocious, almost overtly declared hatred of this man, in evidence from the very first day.

They were shopkeepers, and it was their duty to pass judgment upon a poet! At long last, we've got one!!! There was nothing more to say, and the sympathetic testimony of God himself would have fallen on deaf ears.

The democratic institution of trial by jury, in which a superior man is delivered helpless to the whims of twelve yokels born to serve him, is so fundamental that the miserable wretch can raise no objection regarding his judges. However deeply he feels, however surely he knows, that each one of them has condemned him in advance, if he's unable to demonstrate that his condemnation profits them directly, he is forced—for his very life is at stake—to appear to take them seriously, and even to implore their mercy, with no hope of receiving it, loathing them all the while.

The Poet acted in his own defense. His lawyer was a spineless, spiritless idiot who'd lost before he'd even begun. The crime was so heinous the sentence was sure to be death. If there was really no way for him to save his neck, he wanted at least a few generous words to be spoken on his behalf. And, however abject they might be, he wanted these vile bourgeois who were sending him to the guillotine to retain a disturbing keepsake of their deplorable justice.

He spoke for close to an hour, with incredible fortitude. He recounted a proud life of suffering, he told of his solitude, his poverty, the quasi-monastic regularity of his day-to-day existence. And now he would perish, victim of the most inexplicable error, for the sole reason that it had been impossible for him to recall and give proof of what he was doing on a certain night three years prior.

He shook this horrifying fate upon his shoulders with gestures like a lion in despair. Hearts, like crystals of compassion which a too powerful vibration would have shattered, split and burst. Sobs were heard around the courtroom, pleading for mercy.

The guilty verdict was only rendered more certain. The most influential figure on the jury, a particularly implacable office skunk and little bigwig of indirect Taxation, had no trouble making his colleagues understand that they should resist being won over by a ridiculous tenderness incompatible with their sworn duty. Now, if ever, was the moment to demonstrate the courage of their convictions, a courage well known to be superior to the so-called heroism of the battlefield, and which consists in beating down the poor and the defenseless with indomitable *resolution*.

Moreover, added a horse-faced pharmacist, it was high-time to have done with this trouble-maker, who seemed to look down on them like something stuck to the bottom of his shoe, and under no uncertain terms should they miss the occasion to instill a bit of respect in these tramps and bohemians.

Finally, a seltzer water distributor—a man of action known for being a crackerjack at the billiard table—made the plain declaration that he could care less about proofs. As far as he was concerned, anyone with a mug like that had to be capable of every crime in the book. If by chance the accused was innocent of the specific offense in question, well, he was certainly guilty of several others they just didn't know about, and even supposing he'd never killed anybody, it was incumbent upon them to put him, in the name of the public good and while there was still time, some place where he could do no more harm. The vehemence of this upright citizen carried the day.

The Poet was unanimously and on all counts declared guilty, without extenuating circumstances, and sentenced to death. He rose to his feet, pale as could be, and in a calm voice spoke these simple words to the members of the jury, who were even paler than he:

"Gentlemen, you've just sent an innocent man to the scaffold. Don't forget it."

It was at this moment that my grocer—yes, you heard me correctly, *my grocer,* who was one of the twelve—perhaps in obedience to some mysterious compulsion or simply believing he was back behind his counter, which in the course of infinity may well come to the same thing, replied with this, under the circumstances, staggering commercial slogan: *"No one's ever had a bad word to say about us!"*

CLVIII

LIFE ISN'T ALL ROSES

Tout n'est pas rose dans la vie.

Would the Bourgeois really like for everything to be roses in what he calls life, or is this Commonplace nothing more than the flat and inoffensive observation of a color manufacturer?

I like the first hypothesis, which is certainly the true one. The Bourgeois requires rose-pink—that's his color. His daughters all dress in pink, and so does his wife, at least until she's sixty or so. And he himself is as pink and merry as a young piglet, so long as business is going well. He insists on seeing everything through rose-colored glasses and wants everything in the world to be rosy. His great aspiration in life is to sleep upon a bed of roses. He's the only person who, after so many poets, still speaks now and then of "the rosy-fingered dawn,"[1] and in fairness it should also be acknowledged that, without him, the always fresh and charming observation that "every rose has its thorn" would have long since been obsolete.

Only an *upstart* bourgeois would call for cobalt blue or Indian yellow. And the true, authentic bourgeois, the one with all his ducks in a row, the *well-born* Bourgeois, following the fashion of *genuine* gentlemen, only tolerates the black of death by moaning about it. How widespread they are, these bourgeois who poison children and starve old men and then, after their demise, want to be rolled out in a pink casket, in the middle of a church hung with pink satin and filled with pink attire, while a cheerful organ churns out *La valse des roses!*...

There can be seen, in one of the great cemeteries of Paris, the tomb of a rich wholesale merchant, who had contracts with the Welfare Department to furnish all the rotten meat consumed in public hospitals at a profit margin of no less than three hundred percent. Here was a man of delicious imagination. Above his putrefying innards sits a painstakingly maintained patch of the most exquisite roses, and, engraved on the marble headstone, these four words: "He loved them so!"

---

1. i.e., of Homer's *Odyssey*.

CLIX

THE GOLDEN DAYS OF YESTERYEAR

Les belles années de l'enfance.

O François Coppée!...[1]

---

1. Perhaps a simple ironic reference to lost innocence, perhaps a sneer at "the poet of the humble," who also authored a sentimental, autobiographical novella, *A Romance of Youth*. The poet François Coppée was one of many friends with whom Bloy would eventually break, usually over money, or some point of pride or politics or religious orthodoxy. Bloy met his future wife, Jeanne Molbech, at Coppée's home, and this most personal of the exegeses, no more than the calling of an old friend's (and enemy's) name, reflects that intimacy.

CLX

THE GOOD OLD DAYS

Le bon vieux temps.

Some say that a period known invariably as "The Dark Ages," as opposed to "The Age of Enlightenment" (that's the name of *our* age), couldn't possibly be good and, the older it is, the less good it must be. Others assert, without sufficient proof, in my opinion, that the *goodness* of a given period is by no means incompatible with darkness and old age.

A third group, to which I belong, boldly contends that this Commonplace should be thrown on the scrap heap, because what we have agreed to call the good old days, namely, I suppose, the Thirteenth Century, was, on the contrary, and *par excellence,* as it were, *the good young days,* the days of strength and love, of light and beauty, while the Twentieth corresponds more and more to days of decrepitude, the hideous and hateful image of the most doddering senescence. But try and tell a trial attorney to re-adjudicate the Fourth Crusade!

CLXI

THE LORD LOOKS AFTER DRUNKS AND FOOLS

Il y a un Dieu pour les ivrognes.

The Bourgeois is especially fond of this one. It's one of those phrases that affirms his eternally renewed desire to spit upon the Holy Face, to defile the Word as much as possible.

"God ordered his angels to carry you in their hands," said the Tempter, "for fear your feet might strike a stone."

Yes, I know, you're going to tell me the Bourgeois doesn't know anything about all that, he has more important things to do than read Saint Luke or Saint Matthew. Indeed, what could the Gospels possibly teach him? *He is altogether infused with blasphemy.* The filth excreted by his fathers makes its way into him naturally, effortlessly, as waste passes from one sewer to another. Some receive it in such abundance they become drunk with it and need to be held up by angels—and what angels!

The development of such an idea falls outside the scope and purpose of the present book, but I hope its consolations won't forever be withheld from me. "It shall be seen," I was writing to some unknown person, "that not a *single one* of the Savior's words, or those of his Friends, has escaped the continuous denials and insults of Christians themselves, and our devout fellow worshippers, one would like to believe, will be happy to learn that always and everywhere they speak like demons."

CLXII

APPETITE GROWS BY WHAT IT FEEDS ON

L'appétit vient en mangeant.

A fine reply to a man dying of hunger:
"Poor wretch, you don't know what you're asking for. If you were to eat, you would want to eat more, and then you would be increasingly dependent on honest folk who would go to ruin themselves without ever managing to satisfy you. A person unable to be left wanting is a person who's always left hungry for more, and one doesn't go begging alms at ten o'clock at night. I should think it criminal on my part, to give you so much as a penny."

Let's set the scene: a snowy evening. Our speaker is a fat man, all flushed in the wake of a delicious dinner. He's just come out of the restaurant and is waiting for his car which traces a market index curve to pull up alongside him.

The hungry man represents any sort of suffering you like, the suffering of any age. The niggard represents nothing more or less than Despair—red, swollen, sputtering desperation.

CLXIII

BANKS ONLY LEND TO THE RICH

On ne prête qu'aux riches.

Why, you ask? Because, replies the registrar of the Justice of the Peace, water always runs downhill (to the river). Since the Pactolus,[1] there's always been something between the rich and rivers. Sometimes this water comes directly from virgin sources up in the mountains. More often it's already been used to wash the dishes or rinse the chamber pots.

The rich, like rivers, receive every last drop, but the word *lend* here is a piece of mockery, for when has there ever been an example of this or that rich person *giving something back?* Thus they become, each in their own way, vast waterways, equal parts liquid sewage and tears of the poor, rolling all the way to the Great Abyss.

---

1. Bathing in the river Pactolus, King Midas rid himself of the golden touch. Gold from this same river was later said to be the source of Croesus' wealth.

CLXIV

THERE'S NO SUCH THING AS A STUPID JOB

Il n'y a pas de sot métier.

Forgive me, there is one. To be a tailor and make clothes for a monk. The habit doesn't make the monk, as everyone knows, and, accordingly, it's impossible to imagine anything stupider than making outfits for a client who, given that he doesn't exist, needs to be *made* himself. The matter, I confess, does not appear fully intelligible.

But what is a monk, after all, if not a man or so-called man whose *job* it is to practice obedience, chastity, and poverty? Precisely the opposite of what the Bourgeois calls life.

How's that for an even stupider job than the one just mentioned? A monk takes no part whatsoever in bourgeois existence, nor does he gain anything wearing an outfit that fails to confer even the tiniest semblance of affiliation with the bourgeoisie! A monk crossing paths with a tailor is probably the most extraordinary, most insane, most comic and fantastical thing imaginable.

CLXV

NIGHT WAS MADE FOR SLEEPING

La nuit est faite pour dormir.

I live in a region, on the left bank of the Marne, which in 1870 and 1871 was ransacked, pillaged, ransomed, plundered, and mistreated by the Germans, in every way and with great particularity, and where it is impossible to find anyone with any memory of it. It's a bit disheartening for a French citizen with a few war stories to tell. As it happens, I had one of my own that wouldn't have been entirely without interest—if only it didn't rely so heavily on souls long since departed!

Given the sort of internationalist sentimentality that would rather we forget the horrific Ravages of that time and instead all kiss and join hands in a show of cosmopolitan forgiveness and universal dung-spreading, I wonder where or if I might find a listener capable of swallowing the anecdote about the three Prussians, sent *ad patres* (in the middle of a night undoubtedly made for sleeping) by their prisoner, a sniper from the Vendée, whom they were conducting to the Prince of Saxony and who was to be brought before the firing squad the following morning.

This nimble-fingered and light-footed captive knew the Commonplaces as well as I, nor was he unaware of the fact that night, in addition to being made for sleeping, also "gives good counsel"[1] to brave men, or that all snipers, like all cats, "are gray by night."[2]

Obviously I'm not going to detail the agility and boldness he was able to call upon then. It would be too painful for those sons of ravished women, those skittish bastards hocking their wares along the same walls where Prussian riflemen gunned down the men who might otherwise have been their fathers. And it wouldn't be the first time I was accused of *exaggerating* and overplaying the horror.

Well then, dear reader. My man was a peerless butcher who would have skinned a lion alive before it had a chance to bare its claws. May that bit of information suffice.

---

1. *La nuit porte conseil.* In other words: "best to sleep on it," though a literal translation is necessary here to complete the series.

2. Another commonplace: *La nuit, tous les chats sont gris.*

CLXVI

OPPORTUNITY MAKES THE THIEF

L'occasion fait le larron.

Sol cognovit occasum suum.[1] "Is that you, Lord? Is it you, at last?" asks the thief upon the cross. "I tell you, truly," replies the crucified Light of the world, "today you shall be with me in Paradise."

This takes place in the Darkness of the Sixth Hour,[2] and the Bourgeois *hanged* himself while the sun still shone.

Post-scriptum. I'd have liked to have found the *opportunity* here for an unending tirade, in which I would have said that the only reason the Bourgeois has money is so he can hand it over, and if he doesn't, he's a thief with neither cross nor Paradise. Judas, less crooked than he, GAVE HIS MONEY BACK before stringing himself up. But try to make anyone understand these things!

---

1. Psalm 103:19. "The sun knoweth his going down."
2. i.e., around twilight or nightfall.

CLXVII

WHERE THERE'S SMOKE THERE'S FIRE

Il n'y a pas de fumée sans feu.

That's right, Bourgeois, even in Revelation, a book in which you are much spoken of.

"And the smoke of their torments shall ascend up for ever and ever: neither have they rest day nor night, who have adored the beast, and his image, and whoever receiveth the character of his name."[1]

I commend you to this place.

---

1. Apocalypse 14:11.

CLXVIII

CHOOSE THE LESSER OF TWO EVILS

Entre deux maux, il faut choisir le moindre.

Yes, without a doubt, but how to tell which is which? The most charitable among us will acknowledge that the *lesser* evil is invariably the one afflicting somebody else, and that this indeed is the one that must be chosen. As moralists have long observed: we never lack for strength to bear the suffering of others.

CLXIX

YOU CAN'T PLEASE EVERYONE,[1] OR
WHAT'S SUITABLE FOR YOUNG LADIES

On n'est pas louis d'or, ou Ce qui convient aux jeunes filles.

You can't please everyone. You're not a gold coin. You're not even a half-dollar. I was made painfully aware of this in Denmark, where I was worthless currency.[2] It's bad enough in France, I don't have a whole lot of trade value here, but over there—if you only knew!

I was living, by special decree of inhuman fortune, in a little town in Jutland to which I expected to leave my bones some day. I had been giving French lessons there, and so far had had three students. I'll only speak of number 2, at least for today. Number 1 would take up too much space and 3 is of no interest.

Monsieur Kanaris-Petersen[3] taught French at a local school and enjoyed the highest esteem. I knew from the first, he told me himself, that the name Kanaris—nothing Danish about it, despite the artifice of the initial K—came to him, whether by direct or indirect transmission, from the famous Greek hero of the war for Independence!...

I never undertook to verify this parentage, but I was astonished to learn, by asking him a few innocent questions, that he was completely unacquainted with those oft-cited verses by Victor Hugo which this admirable corsair inspired.

May I never again cross paths with such precious vanity, such complete

---

1. Literally, "You're not a gold coin."

2. Léon Bloy lived with his family in Denmark on two separate occasions. He refers here to the second, a 17-month stay in 1899–1900. —J. P.

3. An actual person, whose real name was Kanaris Klein. See Bloy's *Journal* for 22 February 1899: "Had a visit today from one Kanaris Klein, a professor of French, who is supposed to be something of a bigwig here. He wants me to give him a few lessons in French literature, to help him better understand François Coppée. There's nothing of the corsair about him, but he claims to be related to the same Canaris Hugo celebrated in *Les Orientales* as having "summoned forth the conflagration." The adolescent Jutlanders admire him as the *Arbiter elegantiarum* around these parts. For a full portrait of this imbecile, refer to my *Exégèse des Lieux Communs*..." —J. P.

and succulent imbecility. Canaris, the Greek Patriot of *Songs from the East*,[4] "summons forth the conflagration"; Kanaris of Jutland calls down rain and ridicule. And what ridicule! One has to have spent time in Denmark, one has to have lived in this country of consummate mediocrity, in order properly to appreciate the tender idiocy of such a hall monitor getting the idea to refashion himself a pirate.

Naturally, such rarefied extraction required the most aristocratic affectations. Monsieur Kanaris Petersen is something like the Beau Brummell of his Podunk Hollow. The young Danes glance over their shoulders at him as he passes, attentive to the speech and gestures of this *Arbiter elegantiarum*.[5]

"And the Lord God said, It is not good that Man should be alone; I'll make a helper suitable for him." No one will be surprised if I add to the preceding that there does indeed exist a Madame Kanaris-Petersen, and that she is by no means unworthy of her spouse. There are no known *palikari* or Moldo-Wallachian conquerors in the lady's ancestry, which is made up predominantly of trinket-sellers and wholesale ironmongers, but it's said she has money and was quite the looker once upon a time. You wouldn't know it at a glance. To me she seemed rather boxy and full of verjuice, which probably helps lend her an air of grandiloquence in this provincial rump-end.

One incontestable fact: an invitation to the Kanaris household means you're in for a roaring good time. Plays and costume balls eight or ten months out of the year, Madame Kanaris having acquired a reputation as a delicious ham, and in a Danish *Saint-Germain des Philistines* suburb like this, shitting one's own bed is generally considered the ultimate expression of Atticism and refinement.

Growing up in the middle of this mess are two little girls whose mother's infanticidal frivolity dresses and undresses ten times a day. What will become of them? It's all too easy to foresee. The Lutheran world is the bastard Satan's empire, in which crime and even filth are run-of-the-mill aspects of life. To set

---

4. Constantine Kanaris (or Canaris) was one of the most famous heroes of the Greek War of Independence. The poem Hugo dedicated to him in *Les Orientales* concludes with these words: *Mais le bon Canaris, dont un ardent sillon/Suit la barque hardie,/Sur les vaisseaux qu'il prend, comme son pavilion,/Arbore l'incendie!* (But like his pennant, flying on the vessels he takes, good Kanaris, whose daring bark is followed by an ardent wake, summons forth the conflagration!) —J. P.

5. See above.

one of these wretched souls free, God would have to displace every last ruin of his dashed creation.

"Our little girls will love dancing, just like Mommy and Daddy do!" So he told me once, this morose cretin who never finishes declaring his vivacity and cheerfulness. What a downward spiral then flashed before my eyes! So, I said to myself, this is what's suitable for young girls! To dance like Daddy and Mommy, with everything such choreography presumably entails. But what is not suitable for them, absolutely not, would be to go to mass, for example, or to do anything decent or generous, whatever it might be.

A year after having left this foul country, I learned that my Kanaris, whose handshakes I steadfastly endured, believing him to be a harmless animal, had gone to such great lengths to do me harm it left him stiff and aching. It's been reported to me he said the following, which I'm repeating here in order to ignite with one last fire those enthusiasts who might have seen me come into this world:

"The house of Léon Bloy is no place for young ladies."

CLXX

CRITICISM IS EASY, MAKING ART IS HARD

La critique est aisée, mais l'art est difficile.

I'm not sure the Bourgeois would go to any great pains defending the idea that making art is hard, but I know he's convinced criticism is easy, and even the easiest thing in the world. This is something he sets great store by. Nevertheless, we'll have to find some common ground. The Bourgeois isn't an ass. Criticism can be quite difficult indeed, when it has to contend with great art—veritable art—such as Bouguereau's[1] paintings or Paul Bourget's literature. Where would we be if any bum off the street were permitted to touch those golden humps?

How easy it is, on the contrary, to judge Verlaine, Villiers de l'Isle-Adam, Barbey d'Aurevilly, Ernest Hello! And when was a critic ever more at ease than when granted leave by Providence to drop his dung on the author of these humble pages?

---

1. William-Adolphe Bouguereau (1825–1905), an academic painter generally reviled by the avant-garde (and Bloy), and whose disdain he reciprocated.

CLXXI

I'M A PHILOSOPHER, OR THE YEAR 40

Je suis philosophe, ou *l'An quarante.*

I humbly beg you, don't ask this tanner whether he belongs to the Ionian school founded by Thales and renovated by Anaxagoras; don't try to work out whether he's a Pythagorean, a metaphysician, a Platonist, or a Peripatetic; whether he's a disciple of Euclid or Antisthenes, of Pyrrhus or Epicurus, Zeno or Carneades; don't indulge in the foolishness of supposing him to be an eclectic, a mystic, a stoic, a skeptic, a syncretist, or an empiricist. Finally, and above all, don't go imagining him to be a Christian of any kind. When he tells you he's a philosopher, all this means, simply enough, is that his belly is full, his bowels are unobstructed, his wallet or change purse is suitably plump, and, as a result, he's as indifferent to the rest of it as he is to "the Year 40"[1]—in other words, he doesn't give two damns.

I've often wondered what to make of this famous *Year 40*, treated with such contempt by the philosophers. Impossible to find any information on it. And yet something out of the ordinary must have happened that year. How do we know? The ephemerides and synoptic tables tell us nothing. Let's just take note that the Year 40 is an extreme point of comparison, a standard of contempt. Maybe the first thing you would have to figure out is what the Bourgeois considers to be the most contemptible thing in the world. But who would dare descend into that abyss? *Cum in profundum venerit, contemnit.*[2]

---

1. The origins of the expression *Se foutre comme de l'An quarante,* which literally means "to care as little about *x* as about the year 40" are uncertain, but it probably derives from the French Revolution, when the sans-culottes used it to mock the anticipated 40-year reign of Louis XVI, who would in fact lose his head before he himself reached the age of 40. Another possible source was Louis-Sebastien Mercier's popular utopian novel, *L'an 2440, rêve s'il en fut jamais,* which described an idyllic society of wisdom and equality, set in a future far too remote for the revolutionaries of the time.

2. Proverbs 18:3. *Impius, cum in profundum peccatorum venerit, contemnit.* "The wicked man when he is come into the depth of sins, contemneth…" —J. P.

CLXXII
JUST THIS ONCE…
Une fois n'est pas coutume.

Bourgeois motto of self-exoneration. All's well so long as the habit doesn't take root. The essential thing is not to kill one's father more than once.

A pastor from around here told me, "I have three thousand bottles in my wine-cellar, and my health doesn't permit me to become a saint." You don't see the connection, neither do I, but there is one, certainly.

CLXXIII

THAT'S THE LAST THING I NEEDED!

Je n'avais pas besoin de ça!

So says the Bourgeois whenever some unforeseen accident overwhelms him or even just confuses him a little. It's a way for him to position himself vis-a-vis God and interrogate Providence with superiority. There are very few adolescents between the ages of 16 and 18 who were never struck—sometimes to the point of bedazzlement—by the kind of innate knowledge the Bourgeois seems to have when it comes to what is suitable to him and what he needs. No other known species of animal, even among the solidungulates, is favored with so sure an instinct. Though of course the bourgeois bloodhound nose is at its most prodigiously manifest when it's a matter of things he *doesn't* need and which, as a result, might cause him some annoyance. Allow me to offer you a remarkable example.

About twenty or twenty-five years ago, I was in a café near the old Saint-Lazare station at around ten o'clock at night, in the company of two likeable buddies, one of whom has since been inducted into the Académie Française, while the other is doing hard labor. If memory serves, we had been drinking a fair bit, and were already thinking of ways to finish the night off in some other establishment, when the door opened with a crash and who should come roaring in furiously but the famous Joséphin Dodécaton, national marbleworker of Petit-Montrouge and inventor of unusable burial chambers...

The great man had lost all control of himself and to us he appeared, not to put too fine a point on it, to have reached the furthest extremes of exasperation.

"That's the last thing I needed!" he kept repeating, grunting like a pachyderm. "That's just exactly the last thing I needed. This sort of thing could only happen to me. It's enough to make you believe there isn't a God up there after all!" Etc., etc.

He nonetheless ordered himself a beer and ended up recounting the whole story. He had missed the 9:55 train and found himself compelled to abandon some deal that would have been highly-remunerative. We were already sufficiently *disturbed* before the unlucky fellow arrived, so we left him to his moaning.

Barely had we reached the street when a frenzied and strangely lugubrious clamor alerted us to the horrifying catastrophe that had befallen the express which Dodécaton had so unfortunately failed to catch. The train had just wrecked not fifteen hundred meters from the station, and most of the passengers were crushed or mutilated.

To the stupefaction of people in the street, who must have thought us stricken mad, we burst into laughter, picturing our sepulture-salesman who was probably still in the café carrying on his lamentations. My pal—the one who didn't become an Academician—pointed out once more the infallible discernment of those who get "the last thing they need."

"Had that fellow been ground up with the rest of them," he said by way of conclusion, "and assuming he could still speak, he'd be making the exact same complaint." Absolutely. The Bourgeois is always right.

CLXXIV

CHILDREN ARE WHAT WE MAKE OF THEM
Les enfants sont ce qu'on les fait.

A comforting maxim, and what a future it cracks open for us! It is no doubt nature's intention that the children of the bourgeoisie grow up to be bourgeois themselves. Sometimes, however, one of them gets away. Then the unfortunate shopkeeper must endure the opprobrium of having a poet for a child. The good news is this happens too rarely for anyone to pay it much consideration. Nature, generally, is obeyed. And so the bourgeois shall always be with us.

But do they make them today like they used to, oh, thirty years ago? Everything depends on the answer to this question. Well then! Dare I say it? It seems to me the Bourgeois is taking a turn for the worse. Admittedly, he hasn't forgotten the major principles. It could even be fairly argued that he adores money more than ever before, while pushing God away with an even firmer hand. In those respects he deserves nothing but praise and exaltation. Only the Bourgeoisie, like any other great thing, must nourish itself on the milk of tradition, and it seems to me it went off the tracks in pursuit of novelty some time ago.

The bicycle and the automobile are tremendously artistic, did you know? and nobody knows where this will all end up. The current flows so swiftly, there's reason to fear that in one or two generations the sons of the bourgeois might all be Albrecht Dürers, or Shakespeares, or Beethovens, and that the Bourgeoisie itself might perish, suffocated by Art. It's my patriotic duty to sound the alarm.

CLXXV

YOU HAVE TO MAKE A NAME FOR YOURSELF

Il faut se faire un nom.

It's not as easy or as clean as making children, but there are so many ways to do it! There's the name Napoléon, and there's the name Félix Potin.[1] These two examples allow me to dispense with a thousand others. It would be puerile to explain the difference between these two kinds of fame, or to harp on the enormous superiority of a man who lived for the sole purpose of making money over a miserable emperor who died in exile. If something is truly great it stays put: Stupidity, Cupidity, Abjection.

When Victor Hugo speaks of "Reputations taking flight, shirts undone, barefooted, bugles in hand, before the Master of Armies,"[2] the beautiful imagery inspires pity in those who remember what radiant and unbloody Marketing was able to make of the names Ménier and Géraudel.[3] Posters on every wall, on the fences around construction sites and vacant lots, on the ceilings of omnibuses and the partitions between urinals, in every country in the world—and there you have the very Book of Life, for bastards who know how to make a name for themselves!

---

1. Potin (1820–1871) was a businessman who ran a mass-distribution retail enterprise.

2. Cf. Hugo's *Les châtiments:* NOX, III (1853). —J. P.

3. Ménier's chocolate and Géraudel's pastilles were famous for using advertising—especially attractive posters—to popularize their products.

CLXXVI

YOU DO WHAT YOU CAN

On fait ce qu'on peut.

Once you've made a few rugrats and managed to make a name for yourself, you've done what you could do and I don't see what more could be asked of you, even if it's the Lord God Himself doing the asking. The famous Commandments of Sinai are only there for optional decoration. What has just been specified is all we have that is solid and certain.

"Once," said the Blessed Angela da Foligno, "when I was plunged deep in a meditation on the death of the Son of God, a voice spoke these words directly into my soul: *I have not loved you in jest!* I felt as though I'd received a mortal blow, and I don't know how I escaped dying... More words came to increase my suffering: *I have not loved you in jest, I have not merely* pretended *to serve you, I have not reached out to you from afar but touched you directly!*"[1]

At this last phrase, the Bourgeois—the true, eternal Bourgeois, the natural born murderer—leaps up screaming:

"*You* touched me! You! You dare to say you've touched me, with your perforated Hands and Feet and your bloody Face and your bloody Sweat and the hue and cry of the Jewish multitude and the supernatural effluence of your prolonged Scourging! *You* touched *me*! Ha! Truly, my poor Man-God, my poor Good Lord of the olden days! Do you even have so much influence on me as a two-bit coin? You didn't want to fool about with your Blessed One, and your Blessed One didn't want to fool about either. Good for you! With me it's just the opposite. I'm a cheerful sort, a joyous fellow, and I don't need your Tears any more than I need your Blood. I was born to do business and have a good laugh, and I don't know the first thing about penitence or ecstasies. You do what you can, I suppose—we're not cattle, after all!

Post-scriptum. The Judge will say, "I was hungry, and you did not feed me; I was thirsty, and you gave me not to drink..."

And a thousand pork-butchers will answer: "Listen, that's all well and good, but Lent puts an awful crimp in our bottom line."

---

1. Bloy quotes from Ernest Hello's translation of Angela of Foligno's *Book of Visions and Instructions*, Chapter 33. The present version is based in part on Hello and in part on A. P. J. Cruikshank's translation from the original Latin.

CLXXVII

ONE...

On...

What exactly does *One*[1] mean to the Bourgeois? This abstraction he's constantly invoking, might it not be the unknown God Himself? No One knows this man, no One loves him, no One has ever seen him, One has seen him often enough. Do you know any more certain or efficacious expressions of disapproval than these? Who holds lightning in his hand? Who gives us life? *One* does. Who's heard of you? Who knows who you are? Who gives you credit? *One*.

Every time the Bourgeois speaks, this mysterious *One* jangles like a bag of money, plunked down on the floor of a neighboring room where *some*one[2] has just been murdered.

---

1. The French pronoun *on* is the grammatical third person neutral and has no exact equivalent in English. Depending on the context, it can mean "someone," or "we," or "they," and often it refers to a more abstract collective person, "one." This last, impersonal usage encompasses the others, but the polysemous potential of the French can only be hinted at in English.

2. Not *on* in this case, but *quelqu'un*, *i.e.* "someone." A specific and not an abstract person.

CLXXVIII
ALL MEN ARE BROTHERS
Tous les hommes sont frères.

See number CL, where I believe I've said all there is to say on the matter.

CLXXIX

ALL OR NOTHING

Tout ou rien.

All, when it's a question of how much to refuse. *Nothing*, when it's a question of how much to give. It's the great primordial law. In practice, this is mitigated according to the circumstances, which are infinite. Sometimes it's even necessary to give everything. You saw something like that in 1870, when the Prussians had their bayonets up the asses of the Bourgeoisie. But the principle stands.

CLXXX

WHAT WOMAN WANTS, GOD WANTS

Ce que femme veut, Dieu le veut.

If your wife wants you cuckolded, O office lackey, the Good Lord Himself wants it. And it's a safe bet she wants it often. Up to you to deal with things accordingly. Still, this is no small lot to shoulder the poor creature with, so it seems to me. Because really, if she *doesn't* want this or that, won't God then have to *not* want it either, and wouldn't that make her the very axis on which the world turns? Or is this sort of pact, between her will and the will of God, declared null and void in cases of negative volition? I can think of so many other difficulties besides! But it isn't up to me to resolve them, is it? Life is enigmatic enough already, without having to disentangle the metaphysical chaos of a bookkeeper's brains.

What amazes me, despite my experience with the capriciousness of accountants, is the sort of respect they have for divine Will, manifested in their impure hearts by the will of womankind.

"O woman, great is thy faith," said Jesus to the Canaanite.[1] "Be it done to thee as thou wilt."

Poor Bourgeois! His Commonplace intones a mystery to shatter the heavens! It expresses, nakedly, the most impatient, most explosive reality, and it cannot so much as be uttered without calling down thunderbolts. If only he knew!

---

1. Matthew 15:28.

CLXXXI

RICH IS THE MAN WHO PAYS HIS DEBTS

Qui paie ses dettes s'enrichit.

I confess my complete lack of experience here. I've paid my debts on a more or less regular basis, sometimes I've paid other people's debts as well, and I can't say I've noticed my share of riches to have significantly appreciated as a result. This probably has to do with the fact that I would hand the money over somewhat gloomily. I had a landlord who more than anything wanted me to share in his jubilation. Not being an especially intellectual type and seeing my lack of enthusiasm, he nevertheless had the inconceivable temerity to serve me, one day when rent was due, the *datorem hilarem*[1] of Saint Paul to the Corinthians—a text the Mother Church reserved (until that day) for the office of Saint Lawrence on his roasting spit—informing all his renters that henceforth and without exception they would be obliged to spill forth their precious metals gleefully.

I've written more than once—and with terrific restraint, the angels know—that the money pocketed by landlords means, a large number of times out of ten, the death of sick people and tiny infants, and I pray you believe me I'm a doctor in the subject.

We were alone, my arrival had gone unseen, and the place was isolated. I split open that joyful man's head and carved off several slices which were then expedited by parcel post to my other creditors, including a priest. This memory is like a ray of moonlight in my life. Indeed, one hell of a debt was paid that day—but I didn't get rich off it…

Out behind the Bourgeois house is a balcony giving on to an abyss. Could be that's the place to look.

---

1. "*…for God loveth a cheerful giver*, etc." Corinthians 9:7. —J. P.

CLXXXII

WHEN THE DEVIL WAS OLD, THE DEVIL A MONK WAS HE...

Quand le diable devient vieux, il se fait ermite.

The devil's old age is one of the Bourgeois' most beautiful inventions. Alfred de Vigny, who fostered bourgeois notions now and then, nonetheless struck upon the idea, in his capacity as a gentleman-poet and romantic, of portraying the Enemy of mankind as a handsome adolescent. This revival of twenty centuries of paganism was carried out around 1830. Virgins and matrons alike, billing and cooing the verses of *Eloa*, sighed voluptuously:

I love you and I'm coming down, but what will Heaven say?[1]

Heaven will say whatever it likes. A fantasy that couldn't last. Today as previously, we prefer to picture him an old man in a hermitage. The main thing, you understand, is to irritate the Church as much as possible, which is to say, to dishonor the devil, old age, *and* hermit-monks, all in one fell swoop.

Have you noticed how happy it makes the bourgeois to be able to degrade a religious conversion in precisely these terms? I'm speaking here, it goes without saying, of a conversion that comes late in life. I suppose a poor old fellow might well be weary, to the point of absolute inappetence and nausea, of the idiocies and rottenness of impiety, and thus take notice of the sacraments at last, though it be in the last minute of the eleventh hour.

Within the instant he's declared senile in the provincial or ecumenical councils of Novelty and becomes, in the eyes of the ladies, some sort of retired old goat.

But if a monk, why a hermit? That is, why an anchorite? Why not the cenobitic life, a communal life? If we're so absolutely set on this poor devil turning out to be *the* Devil, we might at least permit him to be *legion*, if that's what makes him happy. That way we'd have a few monasteries, a few charterhouses full of old demons, where the swines of Civil Service, Commercial Enterprise, and Real Estate could come in good conscience to have themselves slaughtered, and which the Sovereign Masters of the various Lodges wouldn't dream of persecuting.

---

1. Alfred de Vigny, *Eloa, chapter III.*

CLXXXIII

WHAT WERE YOU DOING IN 1870?

Que faisiez-vous en 1870?

The question, so common still today, will make no sense to the coming generation. Having resolved to be done with these Commonplaces, which begin to nauseate me, and forced as I am to omit a rather large number of them, it seemed to me that this one could expressively encompass them all. At bottom, the Commonplace is a kind of escape hatch for fleeing whenever danger rears its head, and never have so many bourgeois taken flight as did in 1870.

Back then it was a tumultuous, howling, and frantic disappearing act, a tremendous panic that emptied houses and entire towns, the way night laborers empty cesspits. It was the rentier's infamous, naive, and paradigmatic fear, crushing the weak in a mad stampede. What it is, today, is a procession down the highway of silence.

What were you doing in 1870? Nonetheless, it was a time when something had to be done, when you should have been doing something, you wretch, if only suffering through dysentery, like Huysmans, in a military hospital.[1] When we were a hundred thousand strong out there in the fields, deprived of fire beneath a sky of ice, deprived of bread in the heart of France since transformed into Gambetta's eldest daughter,[2] deprived even of the enemy before whom we had never been lined up, maybe then we had a right to make certain inquiries, and to ask the well-dressed and well-fed just what *they* had been doing—in their now-soiled underwear. The answer, sometimes, was humorous, and would often be lost in a grumbling of bellies, like the day we sent the only son of a notary from Château-Gontier into the Mayenne. Today, I repeat, it's the highway of silence. Go ask those great men of ours, fifty years and up, what they were doing in 1870...

The date has become a kind of outline for all the posturing of contemporary ignominy. It signifies every cowardice, every shame, those already committed

---

1. See J. K. Huysmans, *Sac au dos* (1880).

2. No longer, that is, the "eldest daughter" of the Catholic Church, as France had been known, but of the republican Léon Gambetta.

and those yet to come. Most perfect of all is the silence, the universal and silent flight which is either being fulfilled or preparing to be. Bicycles and automobiles are precautionary measures taken in light of an infinite collapse, which the debacle that took place thirty years ago has only modestly prefigured, a timid prognostication offered with downcast eyes. Collapse of bodies or of souls? Nobody knows. Quite probably both. But how to conceive of this world in flight, this mass of deserters, this flood of the horrified…?

At the moment of this writing, a stone's throw away from me, a very poor man is dying. I tried to save him, tried to persuade him to ask for a priest. Since he's no longer able to make himself understood, the family spoke to me of his opinions, which are apparently invincible, and what do you know but all of a sudden I recalled a Commonplace[3] which until just then I'd inexplicably forgotten. The dying bastard's *opinions!* O merciful crucified Savior!…

Not so many days ago, they celebrated Victor Hugo's centenary. It was nice, Hanotaux[4] gave a speech, there was a Crowning of the People's Muse and not an ounce of hypocrisy. Talk about a great man really getting what's coming to him in his own home town! Oh, he had opinions about that as well, and it's amazing how useful Gabriel's jaw-wagging must have been to him! Truly, you'd almost believe that all these suffering imbeciles, all these infinitely pathetic idiots, actually knew where they wanted to go!

To get back to my dying neighbor, he's one in a multitude, nothing more, and I have absolutely no idea where the man was or what he was doing in 1870. I don't even know if he was, at that or any other time, a man. It's enough for me to know that, at the present moment—probably his last—he belongs to the thirty million renegades registered by the so-called French Republic, the purpose of whose canticle is to spit in the Face of God.

I undertook this Exegesis longing—with all my soul, God knows—for the Bourgeois to be silent. His Commonplaces were, in my estimation, a dirty and hideous form of death-dealing. Now that I'm nearing the end, however, it occurs to me—apropos of 1870 and the eternal question with no answer—that bourgeois silence is no less homicidal than bourgeois speech. And the Bourgeois has so many ways of producing silence!

A friend in danger implores him for protection… silence. The Redeemer

---

3. See xx above.

4. Gabriel Hanotaux again. See also XXIII, LVII, LXXXIX, & CLII.

in agony asks him for drink... silence. The Mater Dolorosa beseeches him take pity, not on others but on *himself*... silence yet again. And now here we have France itself, France in its entirety, France who in earlier days had conquered the world, a France now bloodied and weeping, this France cries out to the Bourgeois: "What were you doing in 1870?"

"*I was dying to take a shit.*"

So answers Émile Zola at last, under the appalling pseudonym of *Jesus Christ*.[5]

---

5. See Zola's 1887 novel, *La Terre*, alternately translated as *The Soil* or *The Earth*, about a rural community in central France. One of the characters, Hyacinthe Fouan, also known as "Jesus Christ," has returned from military service in North Africa to a life of drink, theft, and dissolution.

EPILOGUE

"What will you do," asks Someone, "when you're put upon the cross?" "I'll dream sweet dreams," answers my little five-year-old Madeleine. "That's what."

LIST OF COMMONPLACES

A Bird Builds Its Nest One Straw at a Time	158
A Book to Keep by One's Bedside	215
A Cushy Job	204
A Poet in His Spare Time	55
A Priest Is a Man Like Any Other	121
A Respectable Woman	219
Act in Good Faith	143
All Good Things to Those Who Wait	194
All in Good Time	166
All Men Are Brothers	246
All Opinions Are to Be Respected	43
All or Nothing	247
All Roads Lead to Rome	83
All Tastes Are Found in Nature	61
All That Glitters Is Not Gold	170
Always Ready with a Joke	128
Ambition Is the Undoing of Many a Great Man	72
Any Friend of Yours Is a Friend of Mine	213
Appetite Grows by What It Feeds On	227
At Least He Didn't Suffer	100
Banks Only Lend to the Rich	228
Be a Self-Made Man	217
Be Practical	53
Blessed is He Whose Suffering Has Passed	99
Burn the Candle at Both Ends	132
Business Is Business	32
Carry One's Heart in One's Hand	216
Carve Out a Niche for Yourself	131
Certain Limits Must Not Be Crossed	65
Chance	182
Cherchez La Femme!	218

Children Are What We Make of Them	242
Children Don't Ask to Be Born	27
Choose the Lesser of Two Evils	233
Criticism Is Easy, Making Art Is Hard	237
Crocodile Tears	215
Die Rich	38
Do As You Should	52
Do Honor to One's Business	130
Don't Count Your Chickens…	134
Don't Play with Fire	175
Even God Doesn't Ask So Much!	15
Every Cloud Has a Silver Lining	193
Every Man for Himself and the Devil Take the Hindmost	122
Every Religion Has Some Good in It	188
Every Penny Counts	199
Everyone Has to Live	82
Familial Honor	89
Forewarned Is Forearmed	117
From Argument Springs Enlightenment	152
Get Back in the Money	81
Get It Over With	147
Go Along Your Merry Way	124
God Is Done Performing Miracles	197
Good Lord	176
Great Sorrows Are Silent	111
Habit Is a Second Nature	91
Have a Lot on One's Plate	206
Have a Warped Mind, Exaggerate Things	190
Have One's Heart in the Right Place	202
Have Some Self-Respect	203
Have Your Head in the Clouds	50
Having Been, You Cannot Be	161
Health Comes First	195
Heaven Is Not Averse to Compromise	119

Hidden Away in the Cloister	137
Hold Out Your Hand	139
Hospitals Aren't Made for Dogs	19
Howl with the Wolves	70
I Could Be Your Father	97
I Deserve to Take It Easy	78
I Don't Claim to Be Any Better Than I Am	76
I Don't Have Any Change	95
I Don't Need Anybody	110
I Don't Want to Die Like a Dog	212
I Want to Sleep Soundly	210
I Wash My Hands of It (Like Pilate)	47
I'll Believe It When I See It (Like Saint Thomas)…	46
I'm a Philosopher	238
I'm No More Foolish than the Next Person	198
I'm No Saint	74
I'm Not Your Maid	107
I'm Speaking to You as a Friend	214
If Only We Knew Everything!	163
If We All Just Put Our Heads Together…	155
If You Don't Show Up, You've No Right to Complain	208
If Youth but Knew and Age Were Able!	162
In an Interesting Situation	56
Indecent People Fear the Light	26
It's Never Too Late to Set Things Right	157
It's Too Good to Be True (The Bride Is Much Too Beautiful)	126
Just This Once…	239
Keep Pace with the Times	57
Killing Time	127
Life Isn't All Roses	223
Little Streams Form Mighty Rivers	159
Live Extravagantly	207
Looking for Trouble Where None's to Be Found	63
Lose Your Illusions	135

Make a Hole in the Moon	131
Make One's Peace With It	148
Make the Best of a Bad Situation	201
Make Yourself Comfortable	92
Marry Well	146
Medicine is a Vocation	42
Money Can't Buy Happiness, But…	80
Money Has No Smell	168
Money Hides	209
More Catholic than the Pope	60
Mounted Firmly Upon One's Principles	54
Nature	177
Night Was Made for Sleeping	230
Nit-Pick	138
No Good Deed	107
No Pleasure Without Pain	93
Nobody's Perfect	22
Not the First One to Come Along	144
Not Worth a Devil	125
Nothing Is Absolute	17
One…	245
Only the Truth Offends	71
Opportunity Makes the Thief	231
Paris Wasn't Built in a Day	84
Poverty Is No Vice	21
Preaching in the Desert (Like St. John)	49
Put Your Money to Work	31
Quo Vadis?	112
Rain and Shine	85
Reason	181
Respect Decorum	142
Rich Is the Man Who Pays His Debts	249
Science	178
Secure Your Children's Future	129

Set Up Shop	150
She Died Like a Saint	103
Some People Have All the Luck	205
Some Truths Are Better Left Unspoken	62
Sow One's Wild Oats	145
Speak No Ill of the Dead	105
Speech Is Silver, Silence Is Golden	77
Suffer Like a Martyr	136
Support the Arts	151
That Which Proves Too Much, Proves Nothing	156
That's the Last Thing I Needed!	240
The Courage of Your Convictions	220
The Dark Ages	184
The Dead Can't Defend Themselves	106
The Golden Days of Yesteryear	224
The Good Old Days	225
The Inquisition	185
The Law Is on My Side	34
The Lord Looks after Drunks and Fools	226
The More the Merrier	169
The Most Decent of Decent People	86
The Perfect Is the Enemy of the Good	18
The Prettiest Girl in the World Can Only Give What She Has	113
The St. Bartholomew's Day Massacre	187
The Sun Shines on Us All	154
The Year 40	238
There Are Two Sides to Every Story	153
There's No Such Thing as a Stupid Job	229
Time Is Money	167
To Will the Ends Is to Will the Means	199
Too Much of a Good Thing…	66
We Can't All Be Rich	37
We'll Know Each Other in Heaven	120
We're Only Human	145

What Do You Expect? We're Only Human!	118
What Were You Doing in 1870?	251
What Woman Wants, God Wants	248
What's Suitable for Young Ladies	234
When the Devil Was Old, the Devil a Monk Was He...	250
When You're Running the Store...	39
Where There's Smoke There's Fire	232
Worldly Obligations	90
You Can't Change the Way You Are	41
You Can't Do Two Things at Once	165
You Can't Expect the Impossible	115
You Can't Have Everything	36
You Can't Live Without Money	30
You Can't Make an Omelette Without Breaking Some Eggs	94
You Can't Please Everyone	234
You Can't Think of Everything	164
You Do What You Can	244
You Have to Eat if You're to Live	29
You Have to Make a Name for Yourself	243
You Mustn't Take Too Dark a View of Things	191
You Only Die Once	98
You Weren't Put on This Earth to Enjoy Yourself	73
You'd Almost Say He Was Sleeping	101
Youth Must Run Its Course	145

www.ingramcontent.com/pod-product-compliance
Lightning Source LLC
Chambersburg PA
CBHW06205828O426
43661CB00112B/1446/J